THE BOYS IN MAROON

The talk of the toon are . . .
The Boys in Maroon

So goes one of the lines of a song sung increasingly as the 1985-86 football season in Scotland wound to a close. Those "boys in maroon" were the Heart of Midlothian Football Club players who smashed all previous Premier League records with a run of 27 consecutive unbeaten League games, and who managed to reach the Scottish Cup Final at Hampden along the way.

In *The Boys In Maroon* John Fairgrieve, himself a lifelong Hearts supporter, traces the story of an unforgettable season for the Edinburgh club. He has been authorised by Heart of Midlothian to write this book and the club will benefit directly from the proceeds accrued from it.

John Fairgrieve has been granted total access to the unique family atmosphere in the club. He has travelled on the team bus with the players, been a guest in the directors' box, wined and dined with the Hearts Executive Club members and downed pints and sung songs with the ordinary supporters who mean so much to the club and whose support has rallied them in this magnificent year.

This book is dedicated to those many thousands of supporters who so loyally follow "The Boys In Maroon".

Hearts pool for the Cup Final:
Back row: Ian Jardine, Whittaker, McAdam, Smith, Roddy MacDonald, Craig Levein
Middle row: Cowie, Watson, Gary Mackay, Kidd, Clark, Berry, Robertson, Alan Rae (physio)
Front: Sandison, Billy MacKay, Sandie Jardine, Alex MacDonald (manager),
Walter Borthwick (coach) Colquhoun and Black

Hearts at Hampden–the players line up for the anthem

THE TALK OF THE TOON ARE...

THE BOYS IN MAROON

HEART OF MIDLOTHIAN:

The Authorised Inside Story
of an Unforgettable Season

JOHN FAIRGRIEVE

Introduction by WALLACE MERCER

MAINSTREAM
PUBLISHING

In conjunction with
HEART OF MIDLOTHIAN FOOTBALL CLUB

First published in 1986 by
MAINSTREAM PUBLISHING COMPANY (EDINBURGH) LTD.
7 Albany Street
Edinburgh EH1 3UG

in conjunction with
HEART OF MIDLOTHIAN FOOTBALL CLUB
Tynecastle Park
Edinburgh

ISBN 1 85158 048 4 (cloth)
ISBN 1 85158 049 2 (paperback)

Typeset in 12 point Garamond by Mainstream Publishing.
Printed by William Collins Sons & Co. Ltd., Glasgow.

Contents

Sponsors

Contributions from the following companies helped make publication of *The Boys in Maroon* possible.

the perfect match

ALL THE BEST FROM SCOTLAND
Marshall Food Group Ltd.
Newbridge. Midlothian. EH28 8SW.

TENNENT CALEDONIAN
BREWERIES LTD

PARK'S OF HAMILTON
LUXURY COACH OPERATORS

ALLOA BREWERY COMPANY LIMITED

James Clydesdale and Associates

LOUDEN

T. & G. Louden (Roofing) Limited
Industrial Roofing Specialists.
11/41 Trafalgar Lane,
Leith,
Edinburgh EH6 4DQ.
Telephone: 031-553 4747.

Scottish
Brewers
Limited

Spicer and Pegler
Chartered Accountants

The Hearts Song

Away up in Gorgie at Tynecastle Park
There's a wee football team that aye makes its mark
They've won all the honours in footballing art
And there's nae other team to compare with the Hearts

H-E-A-R-T-S
If you cannie spell it then there's what it says
Hearts, Hearts, Glorious Hearts
It's down at Tynecastle they bide
The talk of the toon are the boys in maroon
And Auld Reekie supports them wie pride

For National caps we can always supply
Like Massey and Walker or Bauld and Mackay
If I had the time I could name dozens more
Who have helped in producing the old Hampden roar

H-E-A-R-T-S
If you cannie spell it then there's what it says
Hearts, Hearts, Glorious Hearts
It's down at Tynecastle they bide
The talk of the toon are the boys in maroon
And Auld Reekie supports them wie pride
This is my story, this is my song
Follow the Hearts and you can't go wrong
Though some say the Celtic and Rangers are grand
The boys in maroon are the best in the land

We've won the League Flag and we've won the League Cup
Though we sometimes go down we can aye come back up
Our Forwards can score and it's no idle talk
The Defence is as strong as the old Castle Rock

H-E-A-R-T-S
If you cannie spell it then there's what it says
Hearts, Hearts, Glorious Hearts
It's down at Tynecastle they bide
The talk of the toon are the boys in maroon
And Auld Reekie supports them wie pride
This is my story, this is my song
Follow the Hearts and you can't go wrong
Though some say the Celtic and Rangers are grand
The boys in maroon are the best in the land

Introduction

by
Wallace Mercer

THE LAST 7 DAYS have been the most traumatic personal experience of my life. During that time Heart of Midlothian Football Club missed out on winning the Premier League Championship by 7 minutes at Dens Park last Saturday and at yesterday's Cup Final they were beaten by Aberdeen. It is difficult to express in words my feelings at this time, having seen the club achieve so much over such a short period of time—yet, at the same time, miss out on the top prizes.

When I was successful in acquiring the majority interest in Hearts in June 1981, the club was within days of closure if new funding had not been found. The re-establishment of this famous institution and the trials and tribulations along the way are stories for another book. What John Fairgrieve, author of *The Boys in Maroon*, is trying to encapsulate is 10 months of activity commencing in August on a pre-season tour in Germany and finishing today in reflection after being defeated in the Cup.

As Chief Executive, I can only try to set the framework within which personal ambitions and desires can be achieved. The close relationship this year between the players and supporters has been absolutely fantastic and they together have created this enormous energy force which took us to the very brink of a tremendous achievement. Although we do not have silverware in the cabinet to judge this season's performance by, we have laid the foundations for a much more stable and positive future for the club. The benefits from this season will eventually be seen in years to come, not only in the financial standing of the business, but also in the facilities and the team which the supporters themselves have helped to create.

Most businesses are judged by their balance sheets and their financial position. When I acquired Hearts they had no finances and a balance sheet which looked like a disaster area. Everyone said I was foolish investing in a business which was virtually in receivership and in an industry which had a poor social reputation, with a club that had a range of problems both on and off the field of play. Season 1985-86, therefore, is a culmination of 5 years of hard work and the coming together of various elements in the club which have been underpinned with the emotional desire of the people who support the club.

The team, obviously, are the people who achieve the success on the field. But for them to be able to produce these results they need to have support, understanding and guidance from many others. My thanks as Chairman, therefore, go to my board of directors, management team and staff who have all assisted in making the players realise ambitions—in some cases ambitions which they had not considered possible. This book, I hope, will provide some understanding to the supporters, be a good read and encapsulate the "thrills and spills" and the "highs and lows" of what has been a most exciting 10 months.

To be at Hampden yesterday with 40,000 Hearts supporters willing the team on was a tremendous experience. The fact that we lost in itself is not important. The style of play and the adventurous soccer played by our young players was a marvel to see. We can only hope that that experience will create an even greater appetite to go on to the next stage.

On arriving back in Edinburgh last night at the Caledonian Hotel, there were 4,000 supporters singing and dancing— obviously delighted at being associated with the club. That is the reward that will give me and my colleagues enduring satisfaction

Hot property. Wallace Mercer (right) with Craig Levein,
Alex MacDonald and John Robertson

in the years to come. This book is for the supporters written by a supporter, as we thought it was important that the story be told. The proceeds of this venture will be reinvested back into their club.

I can only state that it has been a privilege to be Chairman of Heart of Midlothian Football Club during this exciting time and, although we all may have individual ambitions, we can only achieve those with the support and goodwill of others. Today I feel emotionally drained, having been at the helm during these exciting times, but already plans are being laid for the weeks ahead so that we can regroup and start the next campaign. One thing is certain—the supporters deserve success. My job, along with the management team, will be to provide the foundation for us to go forward. It is necessary at times when you are feeling low to have the energy supplied by others. This gives you the confidence to motivate your colleagues to even higher ideals and ambitions.

As I stated earlier, the club was financially and socially redundant in June 1981. The one item that was not on the balance sheet and has been our strongest asset since that date has been the mobilisation of the supporters to provide Heart of Midlothian Football Club with the financial resources and energy level necessary to take on the "Big Battalions" in Scottish Football. The aim has always been the reinstatement of the club back to some stature in the Scottish game—that has been achieved over the last 10 months and is a more satisfying prize than any Championship or Cup.

We now have the foundations and a scale of support which is second to none outwith Rangers and Celtic. The responsibility, therefore, of the directors and management is to maintain our progress and ensure that this opportunity now provided to us, is not wasted. The provision of a successful family club based on no political or religious bias in an environment which brings pleasure to the community and respect to the city is the overriding aim of myself and my directors.

I hope you enjoy this book and experience some of the flavour and excitement of what has been a most exciting journey.

A. WALLACE MERCER
CLUB CHAIRMAN
Sunday, 11 May 1986.

Setting The Scene

IT WAS NOT only a compliment to be asked to write this book of the Hearts, 1985-86. It was, I confess, something of a surprise. Only a few years ago I suggested to a couple of million or so readers, that, if anybody wanted to turn Tynecastle into a car park then I, for one, would have no special objections.

It will be remembered, no doubt, that Forfar knocked Hearts out of the Scottish Cup that year. Hearts weren't doing very well in the League either, and humiliation at the hands—or feet—of such an insignificant club as Forfar seemed to me to be the last straw. This is not intended to be insulting to Forfar, by the way. But it can hardly be denied that the place is rather better known for loons munching bridies than for football.

Naturally, and quite fairly, I have been reminded of my statement about once a week ever since. Such reminders often take the form of an invitation to be the official car-park attendant. I smile wanly, and will, I trust, continue to do so.

But all that is surely forgiven if not forgotten by now. What we are talking about is the season just ended and there's plenty to talk about. As the undefeated games piled up into a record-breaking statistic, so did the fans start rolling back in their thousands to Tynecastle. Hearts have been well supported, true, for more than a century, but for some time the support had been more in spirit than in presence. People were always interested to know how the Hearts had got on. They weren't paying to find out.

Season 1985-86 has surely changed all that—as near to permanently as things can be in football. The real lesson of the season is not that Hearts won so many matches. It was the manner in which the matches were won. By established tradition that has always counted for a great deal with Hearts supporters. Should anybody doubt that, one need only remember the tremendous crowds that once watched at Tynecastle in seasons long gone, when the team won nothing at all.

Hearts are now a remarkably fit team. It is the obvious reason—apart from an unquestionable determination—why they're still going strong when the opposition is struggling. But fitness is only one aspect of it, however important. Hammer-throwers are fit. Sprinters are fit. Boxers are fit. Hearts use their fitness as a basis for playing entertaining football. A team can win without playing attractive football. Hearts combine both, and that's why they have been one of the ten best-supported clubs in Britain.

Car parks aside, I suppose I do have some qualifications for compiling a chronicle of the season. My first look at Hearts was just before the war. Being not much more than a babe-in-arms, of course, I can't remember much about the games, but I do remember Tommy Walker, Andy Black, Willie Waugh, Jimmy Dykes and big Duncan McClure. Those, as they say, were the days. But better days than now? I doubt it, although the crowds—mainly for social reasons—were larger. There wasn't any racing on the box then.

Moving on, we come inevitably to the Cup-winning team of 1956. Nostalgia is all too apt to cloud judgement and it would be odious to compare that side to the lads of today. Similarly, the side of 1957-58, with its goal-scoring record that cannot be equalled. There may have been some superior individual players in the 1950s and in 1959-60, when the title last came to Tynecastle. I would question whether the *teams* as such were superior. Certainly the atmosphere around Tynecastle was nowhere near as happy as it is today.

Early season first-team squad

There have been bitter disappointments, and I'm not even talking about Forfar now. The championship was flung away in 1964-65, and it has been estimated that Hearts lost half of their support afterwards. For that title was lost badly, by unimaginative tactics, to a team that couldn't have been more astonished by success. Then there was that match in 1973 when Hibs scored four breakaway goals and three more that were blatantly off-side. Eddie Turnbull came into what was then the tea-room at Tynecastle to have a chat with me after the game, but he was not offering any consolation. He did offer me a snowy-white handkerchief, with green borders, in order that I could dry my eyes, as he put it.

I fancy we have had our moments of retribution over Hibs since. There will be many more. It is possibly now in the minds of those who read this that I am not neutral. This would be a highly accurate assessment of the situation. I am not neutral. I have no intention of ever being neutral. Neutrality, so far as I am concerned, is for those with neutral minds.

That must be qualified, even adjusted, I suppose. When Real Madrid beat Eintracht Frankfurt in 1960, Hampden Park was fairly well filled up with neutrals. All appreciated the gorgeous football played by BOTH teams. But that was a one-off.

The football fan does not live by European Cups alone. He lives week after week, and he argues, debates, discusses, and gets into fights over the club he supports. It's a pity he should get into fights, unless he wins, but that's the way it is. (Incidentally, even if he does win, he should not have got into fights. I have no interest in being labelled as a man of no responsibility.)

With any luck at all, this book may be bought, if not actually read, by Hibs supporters. They may buy it in order to burn it, to prop up the dodgy leg of a table, or to throw it at Walter Kidd on New Year's Day. That is their privilege. And I stress that some may even read it, even if they tend to be puzzled by any word of more than one syllable. We would be wrong to blame them for this. It is not their fault. It is the way they have been brought up. I have always been charitable in this. Where I was raised, within shouting distance of Arniston Rangers, it was not unknown to be in the company of Hibbies. I always thought we treated them with compassion, especially when they asked us what a mirror was for. They could never quite understand mirrors. They preferred coloured beads.

But I do not wish to be unkind. In the days approaching the climax to the season, I was quite amazed, almost touched, by the good wishes pressed upon me by people who were well-known for their support for the Hibernian Football Club. One thinks of big Robert MacPherson, who owns that otherwise excellent establishment, La Coquette, in Rose Street. One thinks of Gregor Cowan, a Hibs director, and of Alan Gordon, who played for both Hibs and Hearts and who swears he has no real loyalties to either . . . and that may explain why he keeps wanting to bet against Hearts in multiples of seven. The last time I took the bet, the money was £7.05, and, I am sorry to say, Alan threw the five pence into the Gorgie Road traffic. No class.

They're still reasonable folk, all the same. They are not too

Celebration on and off the bench against Hibs

bright, but, I repeat, they are not necessarily to be castigated for that. All I would insist upon is that when Hibbies start talking about how much they want an Edinburgh team to win—be that team Hibs, Hearts or Meadowbank—they are lying in their teeth. I say this because that is how I would feel were the situations reversed. Well, it takes one to know one.

It is more profitable, I feel, in this book, to mention a few, a very few, of the great Hearts supporters I know. They are not all like John Frame, official and built in with the bricks. John takes some beating.

There's no reason why I shouldn't start with Pilmar Smith, who became a director of Hearts soon after Wallace Mercer put up the money that was to save the club from threatened extinction. Pilmar is Hearts all the way through and he reckons an hour away from Tynecastle as an hour lost. I have to mention Davie Mowat, who used to serve up memorable meals at the old Hearts Social Club and who is now doing something similar at the Press Club. Davie, the club manager, does not go to every Hearts game. That is, quite simply, because he believes his heart—A1 at the last check, incidentally—can't stand the suspense. When he does watch the lads, he turns his head away if the ball is in the Hearts' half of the park. When Bill Barclay, a comic of repute, comes into the Press Club, Davie will not serve him in the event of a Hearts' defeat. Bill, who has been known to remember the names of the so-called "Famous Five", was served with reasonable frequency in the season just ended.

Then we have the West brothers, Alan and Roy. Alan, cured of a totally incomprehensible tendency to rugby—to Heriots, for God's sake—is now back to his Tynecastle roots. Roy was never away from them. Nor was their uncle Harry, who in his dedication to the club almost makes me look like a Hibbie.

Of course, there are so many more. I can only say a word about those of my immediate acquaintance. Tens of thousands will not, I trust, feel left out. We're all in the same family, after all.

But that leaves two, above all. Willie Smith and Dave Speed, who compile the programme and keep the club history up to date. Without them, this book could not have been published.

Man for Man: The Players

IT'S THE TUESDAY before the League game at Dens Park, the game which will certainly decide whether or not the Heart of Midlothian Football Club will be champions. By normally accepted standards, Tynecastle should be as tense as any tight-rope, nerves should be jangling, tempers should be not so much frayed as at breaking-point. At least Alex MacDonald and Sandy Jardine should be snarling at people, and so should Walter Borthwick, that very highly qualified SFA coach. Outsiders should be walking around on tip-toe, for fear of disturbing the finely-tuned temperament allegedly synonymous with pro-fessional football men with so much to gain and so much to lose.

In the players' lounge, however, Sandy Jardine was concerned only by the lateness of one of the young lads who had been sent out for filled rolls and cups of soup. The lad arrived eventually with a loaded tray. "We were thinking of sending out a posse," said Sandy, and the part-time waiter, who, for all we know, could play for Scotland some day, grinned.

Walter Borthwick looked about as nervous as Perry Como. Sandy and Alex MacDonald were giggling like schoolkids over some private joke, and I'd just like to think it wasn't about me, but it's hard to tell with that pair.

"You been drinking?" I asked, wishing to clarify the point right there and then. "I mean, it's only half-past-one in the afternoon, give us a break."

"Ach," said Sandy, "you're just jealous. No, not a drop. Unless coffee. Listen, you're talking to perfectly trained and dedicated athletes here."

Alex grabbed one of the cheap footballs lying in the corner, the £7 versions which the players readily sign for the fans. He indulged in some fairly impressive keepy-uppie. Well, it impressed me anyway, although his colleagues were less than lavish in their praise.

"You can play none," said Sandy.

"You never could," said Walter.

"Watch it," said Alex. "Remember who's the manager around here." He added, for my benefit, "See the pressure, it's murder."

My idea was to ask them their opinions of the first-team players but the problem was to keep them serious. And so, I am obliged to warn readers that the following pen-pictures must be seen as punctuated with certain ribald comments not normally heard at after-the-match press conferences. Perhaps I should warn the players concerned, too, but they're a happy bunch and I don't think they'll be bothered much. We'll begin, not unreasonably, at the beginning, with the goalkeeper.

Henry Smith has been busy proving this season that, without a reliable last line of defence, no team can even hope to succeed. It would be very easy to make out a case that he should have earned some sort of international recognition, but it's not too late for that. He has just turned 30 and has been at Tynecastle since 1981, his previous clubs being Frickley Athletic, Winterton Rangers and Leeds United. It's no surprise to hear him extol the virtues of Gordon Banks, his boyhood hero and one of the finest goalkeepers of modern times, anywhere.

Henry is very much an extrovert on the pitch. He grabs a difficult shot, holds it as if he owned the ball, almost as if he were taunting the opposing forwards. Could there be a touch of arrogance there?

"Not at all," says Sandy Jardine. "It's just that Henry is

Safe in Henry's hands against Rangers
16 November 1985

surprised he held the ball in the first place."

Walter Borthwick rates Henry enormously, especially with a challenging cross-ball. "He has fantastic agility," says Walter.

"That's right," says Sandy. "I've never met any player with such a range of movement with his muscles. He's so flexible. I'm telling you, he could put his foot on your shoulder and not bend his leg. He can pick up the ball without bending his knee."

"Yes," said Alex, "especially when he's picking it out of the back of the net.

Walter Borthwick praises Henry's improved maturity and powers of concentration. Sandy agrees. "He's been getting more and more confident all the time. But it is confidence, not conceit. There's no chance of anybody getting big-headed at Tynecastle."

As a personality off the field Henry is nothing like his on-field image. There is no more reserved player at the club. And nobody at the club is more willing to help out, visiting sick children in hospital and doing other charity work.

Walter Kidd has been on the Tynecastle staff longer than any other player but, at 28, he is still some way from being pensionable. I often wondered why he was captain, when the assistant-manager, Sandy Jardine, was playing in the same team. Wouldn't there be some conflict of authority, shall we say? It can't be easy, I'd have thought, for the captain to bawl out the boss on the park when that same boss, in conjunction with the manager, can decide on the next team selection.

"No. No conflict," says Sandy. "Anyway, Walter's one of those lucky captains. He wins the toss. Half the time, anyway."

Alex MacDonald balances that with a more serious comment. "You can't have too many captains on the field," says Alex. "What we want is everybody shouting at each other."

Well, I should have guessed as much. The habit of loud and mutual disagreement—or well-meaning advice—is one nurtured and long encouraged at Ibrox, where the manager and the assistant-manager learned so much of their trade. Indeed it's not so much a habit as an ingrained tradition. It's not necessary to compromise on loyalty to Hearts, to remember with awe the way

Walter Kidd collects the Tennent's Sixes Trophy

lads like George Young and Willie Woodburn used to tell their team-mates precisely what they thought of them, at all times. Many a current Hearts fan will recall the day at Tynecastle when Willie Bauld made Bobby Brown look somewhat foolish with a long, looping 30-yard shot. And Bobby, no mean goalie, will not forget what Willie Woodburn said to him immediately after. What "Ben" did NOT say, was: "Oh, dashed hard luck, Robert, but don't take it to heart."

Another important point about the captaincy, of course, is the fact that somebody such as Walter Kidd can provide a link between playing staff and management. "And just as important," says Alex MacDonald, "is the way Walter typifies the spirit of the team. His kind of enthusiasm is infectious."

"He's real up-and-at-'em stuff," says Sandy.

Walter Borthwick adds: "He seems to run awkwardly, but don't let that fool you. His elbows are going all the time and he's hard to put off the ball."

"What I like about Walter, too," says Sandy, "is the variety he brings to the game. There's this unpredictability. I mean, you never can tell where his passes will go. He likes to bring the fans into the game, doesn't he?"

Meanwhile, Walter Kidd, nine years with the Hearts, is very much one of the boys despite any burden the captaincy may bring. "A real personality," Alex says, "and always buys his round. He's had several nicknames here, like 'Bald Eagle' and 'Biggles'. Don't ask me why he gets these names. Maybe because he doesn't like flying. Another thing, his gear is unbelievable."

"Yes," Sandy chips in, "just like his crosses."

There's another club, a very exclusive one, of which the big-hearted Walter Kidd is a member—or at least, very soon will be. He is to become only the fifth Hearts player in the club's history to receive a testimonial match. The other four are Tommy Walker, Willie Bauld, John Cumming and the present manager himself, Alex MacDonald.

Walter arrived at Tynecastle from Link's Boys Club and Newtongrange Star, and a couple of months later he was making his debut in a friendly against East Fife. You can tell that he is certainly something of a character when he lists his likes and dislikes. Well, there can't be much wrong with somebody whose favourite TV programme is *Only Fools and Horses* and who says that the person he would most like to meet is John Robertson's bank manager. If he isn't kidding when he says that his favourite colour is grey then he should be.

George Cowie has just turned 25, comes from the little fishing town of Buckie, and hasn't had much luck in the last two years or so with injuries. Not much good luck, that is. In March of this year, he said with some feeling: "I've spent more time with our

Conroy's tackle on Cowie earned him a booking
26 April 1986

physio, Alan Rae, at hospital than I've spent at Tynecastle, in the last 15 months." But injuries or no injuries, nobody would question George's value to Hearts, whom he joined three years ago after having played with Buckie Rovers and West Ham. Walter Borthwick admires his speed in the tackle, and his powers of recovery and, of course, his adaptability.

Sandy says: "He's a bampot, he must be, he likes fishing." However, there's reason to believe that this assessment is less than accurate. The mere fact that he comes from Buckie doesn't automatically mean he should like fishing. Or fish. (In fact, George's favourite food happens to be fish and he prefers golf and snooker to fishing anytime.)

"Aye," says Sandy with pretended reluctance, "he's not a bad lad, really. He has great stamina, you know, and I do like his attitude. He'll play anywhere you put him and he won't let you down. He's a happy-go-lucky sort of soul and I've met very few lads who are better-natured. Another thing, his form has improved quite a bit since we found out he needed contact lenses."

George's almost-legendary good nature is paralleled by his good manners and, predictably, he includes bad manners among his active dislikes. Not so predictably, he doesn't own a car, although by now he should certainly be well able to afford one. When asked to specify whom he would most like to meet, George says, "Miss World", and there seems no good reason to suppose he doesn't mean it.

Brian Whittaker takes a fair share of banter from Messrs MacDonald, Jardine and Borthwick and it's good to know that he won't resent one word of it. That's the way he is. Nor, to be frank, would he have any right to do so . . . considering his own penchant for winding up his team-mates at every possible opportunity.

"He's good in the air," says Walter Borthwick, "just so long as nobody's jumping with him."

"No, no. He's a really stylish player," says Sandy Jardine, and we wait for the barbed postscript but, at that point, there is none.

Brian Whittaker
Hearts v Clydebank, 26 April 1986

It is a temporary respite for big Brian.

"He always looks for improvement," says Alex MacDonald, "and there's no doubt he is finding it. That has a lot to do with the full-time training here. He wasn't very long with Celtic, and he was only part-time with Partick Thistle. He has a fine left foot, and I'd say he is an excellent athlete. Mind you, he has one or two bad habits which he'll have to get rid of, and one of them is not buying a drink for the manager."

"And he's fast," says Sandy. "More to it than that, he makes his mates run faster, too. That's when he starts telling them his rotten jokes, and they'll do even-time just to get away from him."

Of all the players at Tynecastle, Brian is probably the only one with the absolute confidence that would inspire an appearance on the public stage—telling jokes, rotten or otherwise. Appropriately enough, he has two boyhood heroes above all—Jim Baxter and John Greig. Appropriately, because Baxter practically invented the word "extrovert"—or the football version of it, anyway—and Greig has no great reputation as a blushing violet either.

Brian's choice of car—a black Turbo—goes smoothly with his attitude to life, but he is not to be taken seriously when he insists that his favourite foods are fish and steak, so long as they are served on the same plate. One also questions his choice of Rock Hudson as his top actor. Likewise, he ponders deeply and decides that his favourite book is Dr Miriam Stoppard's *Book of Pregnancy*. By now, readers may have some idea of what Brian's colleagues are obliged to tolerate. I'm still wondering whether he means it when he says that the person he would most like to meet is Enoch Powell.

Kenny Black was with Rangers and Motherwell before coming to Tynecastle two years ago. "It was at Ibrox that I noticed him," says Alex MacDonald, "and I made up my mind that if he ever became available, then I'd be definitely in the market for him."

But it has been a difficult season for Kenny in many ways. His enthusiasm in the tackle has not always earned the blessing of referees—well, you know how finicky some referees can

Kenny Black

be—and, as a result, he has been "sitting on" nine disciplinary points for months. One more and he would have been away, as they say. Naturally, this realisation has tended to inhibit him on the field, perhaps not always consciously but noticeably. Alex MacDonald puts the point rather pithily. "The only thing Kenny's kicked for months is the kids in the nursery across the road."

Personally speaking, I have to doubt whether Kenny has really been kicking kids in the nursery, although his favourite TV programme is *Minder* and his top actors are Clint Eastwood and Charles Bronson. Moreover, he has been regular enough in the first team. Joking aside, he's a pleasant big lad, still only 22, and has the perception to name Donald Ford as the player he admired most, when in his teens.

The main thing is, he earned his first-team place while simultaneously curbing that natural enthusiasm, which is no easy achievement. He must surely have been greatly relieved—well, I know he was—when, eventually, he realised that he would be eligible for a role at Hampden.

Walter Borthwick praises the way Kenny keeps his game simple yet so effective. "He puts away a good pass, and he's another whose attitude is good. In saying that," adds Walter, "I have to say, too, that there are no players with bad attitudes at Tynecastle. If they didn't fit in with the way we think, I don't think they'd be here very long."

Alex MacDonald looks up and nods his head in agreement.

Sandy Jardine says: "Kenny, he'll get you banned from anywhere. He doesn't even miss a sing-song with Pilmar Smith, and that's something you should hear." Sandy shook his head sadly, and I gained the definite impression that we weren't talking about a Sinatra-Crosby duet here.

"His discipline has improved, though," says Alex.

"Aye, he only gets booked once a week now," says Sandy.

Kenny himself is an uncomplicated character, who doesn't bother with gloomy introspection. His ambition is to be as happy as he can and, at 22, that's as honest an ambition as anybody is entitled to have.

Craig Levein was Scotland's Young Player of the Year in 1985, which was a selection that ought to have surprised nobody. This season he was included in the Scotland squad to play Holland in Eindhoven, but was forced to call off because of a slight injury. It was a blow to him, justifiably so. But anybody who knows football takes it for granted that that disappointment is bound to be compensated for, many times over. In fact, there are many good judges—and not all wearing maroon spectacles—who take the view that Craig deserved some international recognition before April 1986, but, of course, that's the sort of thing all fans like to argue about.

"The boy is just class," says Sandy Jardine. "He's the second-best sweeper at the club." The initiated, about 30,000 of them, will not have missed this point made by Sandy, who likes to be a sweeper himself. He's not bad at it, either.

Walter Borthwick reckons that Craig is such an excellent all-round player that he can't think of any weakness in his make-up.

Alex MacDonald says: "It's certainly not a weakness for a player to know that he's still learning. He's the kind of player who will *always* know that he's learning, no matter how long he stays in the game. And that'll be a long time. He's only about 22 now."

"No weaknesses," snorts Sandy. "That'll be right. How about the time he was sick on one of our best carpets?"

At this point, and taking into account Sandy Jardine's well-known capacity for taking the mickey out of one and all, it should be noted that professional footballers do, on occasion, have a drink. Naturally, this is not something widely publicised, for obvious reasons, but I'd like to think that even the most straight-laced fans would not blame the lads for letting off steam—at the right time.

A few pints on a Saturday night, whether the game has been won or lost, does help players to relax. They don't *need* it. They like it. Their inhibitions are shoved into the background and the strain of playing for bonuses—unhappily unavoidable, these days—is lessened. It's really called letting off steam, and it is most certainly not unprofessional. It becomes unprofessional

Craig Levein
Hearts v Clydebank, 26 April 1986

only when it affects training or match performance, or when it is indulged in at the wrong time—which is just about any time between Saturday and Saturday—and gives the club a bad image. And that is something Hearts need never worry about.

Meanwhile, Craig Levein's fitness is equal to his talent, which is saying something. It is one of my small regrets that I did not get down to the bookies fast enough when the Professional Footballers' Sprint Championship was held at Meadowbank. Craig was only slightly odds-on, which made him the best bet of the decade, apart from the fact that they'd never find Shergar.

Alex MacDonald is ever more impressed by that willingness to learn, to discuss tactics, to evaluate opponents before and after a game. "And we don't mind him going forward. The sweeper bit doesn't matter then, because he's so fast he's guaranteed to get back in time if anything goes wrong. Apart from that, our tactics are geared to this kind of adventure. We talk about it a lot, and Craig talks about it, as much as anybody."

Craig was born in Dunfermline 22 years ago and it is a source of wonder to very many scouts how Hearts collared him from Cowdenbeath in November 1983. It is not a source of wonder, however, to anybody who appreciates the way that the MacDonald-Jardine-Borthwick triumvirate can recognise a potential that was previously unrecognised. When Craig came to Tynecastle, most supporters asked: "Craig who?" And there was some resentment about what was thought to be the management's lack of ambition. There is no resentment now.

The day after I had a chat with the above-mentioned trio about the Hearts playing staff, there was a story published about a very substantial offer made for Craig Levein by Tottenham Hotspur. The offer was quoted at a bit over £600,000 which, as most of us would agree, buys a right good few pints of heavy at the Diggers, Mathers and the Centurion, among other places. At the time of writing this book, I cannot tell how the offer was received by Hearts but, and I speak as one who is known to have had one of those pints of heavy, notably at Mathers, I would hope it is rejected out of hand.

There are at least two good reasons for my attitude, and

Wallace Mercer can say what he likes—and will! First, Levein, together with Henry Smith, is too important to lose at this time. Second, if Hearts must, and I repeat MUST, give way to the blandishments of English money, then there are others who can also be sold for a great deal, and who can be more easily replaced. Yes, and a third reason, which, I am sure, has not escaped Mr Mercer's notice. If Craig Levein is worth £600,000 now—before he has worn a Scotland jersey—what will he be worth in 1987?

Craig is a big, outgoing lad, who likes a bet, a glass of wine with his steak and, whether one believes it or not, the TV programme *Dallas*. Dare we suggest the character with whom he identifies in that soap-opera to end all soap-operas? Let's hope it is JR, and not some wimp like Bobby Ewing. (We should not toss aside the possibility of a resurrection for Bobby, some day.) No, JR seems favourite or, as a second-favourite, that really nasty piece of work, Cliff Barnes. Craig will not, I hope, take the comparison to heart, unless he remembers that, in *Dallas*, only JR and Cliff matter. Craig is lucky. He is one of many at Tynecastle who matter.

Anyway, despite a talent worth hundreds of thousands of pounds, he remains a level-headed lad, who says that the highlight of his career so far was the goal he scored against Hibs in the season before last. Should he wish a seconder to that motion, there would be quite a long queue. He insists that maroon is his favourite colour and he is not the sort of person who would say such a thing if he didn't mean it. Being fond of a gamble now and then, he would like to meet Steve Cauthen some day.

"Yes," says Alex MacDonald, "but that doesn't mean the games in the team bus can have more than £1 stake." The manager ponders for a moment. "Unless," he adds, "I get my percentage."

Neil Berry may not be unique in that he brings an absolutely spontaneous compliment from Sandy Jardine—who tends to disguise compliments in cynical clothes—but he is certainly one of a small number. "That Neil Berry," says Sandy, "if you're

Neil Berry

going over the top, if you're going into a really hard situation, he's the boy I'd want to have alongside me. I'll be a bit less dramatic than that in a minute, though I still mean what I'm saying. If it's a 60-40 ball and Neil has got the 40%, he'll win it."

"He's quick and he's aggressive," says Alex MacDonald. "He's intelligent, a true professional. He knows what he can do, and, maybe as important, he knows what he can't do. That's not to say he won't get any better, because he will. What I mean is, he knows his strengths and he plays to them. You'd be surprised how many good pros don't, or can't do that."

Sandy adds that Neil is also a Hearts fan, through and through. "And, as he learns all the time, he does the right things at the right time, he won't try anything too fancy, for he knows that there are others who are likely to be better than he is at that game. So he gives them the ball . . . but he'll give them the ball at the right instant, as best he can. He doesn't shirk responsibility."

Neil was 23 in April, and came to Hearts from Bolton Wanderers in December 1984. He has rapidly established himself as one of the most-admired players—especially by the fans—at Tynecastle. His position in the team means that he is likely to lack glamour. It doesn't mean, by a long chalk, that he is overlooked.

He says he likes snooker, squash and golf, and, as with almost every footballer ever born, prefers steak to any other food. One refers, reasonably enough, to British-born players, and not to the French, with their yard-long menus, or to the South Americans... all that spicy nonsense.

It is fashionable for supposedly trendy folk to sneer at the classic diet of the football player—prawn cocktail, well-done steak and gateau—but why should lads of that age be expected to get into the *Cordon Bleu* stuff? I make this point as one who knows. I have criticised the football menu myself, in the past, and, frankly, all that makes me is a snob. At least I've got the sense to know it. Given the choice, I'd be trying a real sea-food cocktail, rare steak and a half-dozen or so Gaelic coffees, but I also have the sense to know that this is not a choice calculated to win the approval of football managers.

Neil, by the way, is pleased to put it on record that his top choice of reading material is *The Broons* and *Oor Wullie*. I regard this as his way of making a joke, and not much of a joke at that. Come on, Neil, behave yourself! If you read Sunday papers, you know very well that the only thing to look at, first and last, is the column on the inside-back page of the *Sunday Mail*.

He says, too, that he loves winning city derby games against Hibs, an attitude which is not only understandable but eminently desirable. Then he goes and spoils it by confessing that the person he would most like to meet is the comic, if that's the word, Billy Connolly.

Gary Mackay joined Hearts from Salvesen Boys Club for a minimum fee. In him Hearts have a very hot property indeed. Even taking wages, substantial, one hopes—and assumes—into account, Gary represents the sort of investment of which the banking house of Rothschild would not be ashamed.

There are not too many around like him. His is the kind of talent which cannot be learned. It can be improved upon, it can be exploited, but it still cannot be learned. That makes him a very lucky young lad by any standards and, fortunately for Hearts, he knows as much. If he wore a hat, which he doesn't, it would be the same size now as it would have been in July 1980 when he signed professional forms at Tynecastle at the age of 15.

Alex MacDonald says Gary's father was a Hibbie, and it says much for the Mackays, senior and junior, that he was allowed to rise above his environment. It says a great deal too for Gary's grandfather who, realising one of life's great truths, took the lad to see Hearts at a very early age. Now Gary's dad is converted, more or less, and there are no family squabbles so far as is known.

"What Gary can do," says Alex MacDonald, "is run at a defence, and defenders hate that. Most of them just don't know what to do, whether to back off, or to have a go, and before they know it it's too late."

Any fan seeking confirmation of that theory, will remember the goal scored by Gary against Clydebank in April . . . the only

Gary Mackay

goal of the game, a crucial goal, a beautiful goal. He *did* run at the defence, feinting to the right, taking two men with him, before rattling a spectacular shot with his left foot into the net from well outside the penalty area.

"He has two good feet," says the manager, "and he keeps the ball close to his body when he runs with it. That takes genuine skill. It's an old-fashioned skill, I suppose, but when you see it, well, you cherish it."

"He was a bit frail, almost delicate, when he came here first," says Walter Borthwick, "and he had to harden up quite a bit to play in the Premier League. But honestly, he must have put on a stone, and it's all muscle."

"Now he knows his weaknesses, too," says Sandy Jardine, "but he still has class. He's like big Craig Levein, he could go all the way in this game. He's not so much shy, he's just a nice big laddie. Very clothes-conscious and not a lot wrong with that. Too many slobs about these days, when you think of it. Well, you never see Gary without his hair-dryer, do you?"

Gary would say that he likes nothing better than beating Sandy in bounce-matches and, if there are no bonuses at stake, he probably does that often enough. He wants, perhaps more than anything else, to play for his country, but remains a Hearts supporter to the bone. Definitely, as Sandy says, a nice laddie.

John Robertson scores goals, and it is tempting to leave it at that. Such a temptation is hereby resisted, and without any bother at all. John is a lot more than a mere goal-scorer. His principal asset is probably panic . . . the panic he inspires in an opposing defence.

He is 21, and we are not going to start comparing him with somebody like Jimmy Greaves just yet, because that would do him no favours at all. Give him two or three years, though, and who knows?

"John Robertson?" says Sandy Jardine. "Away, he's a work-horse." Sandy says that knowing full well that to call wee John a work-horse is like calling Sinatra a singer. But that's still how it goes at Tynecastle. There's lots of respect, lots of admiration, but no adulation. When John scored that first goal against Dundee United at Tannadice, he came back to the dressing-room and was told, in chorus, that it was nothing more than a fortunate mis-kick.

"But he does strike the ball well," says Alex MacDonald. "That goal at Tannadice, that was his left foot and no, of course it wasn't lucky. It was timing and it was technique. Some goals are scored by a hopeful swipe from anywhere and the English TV commentators bawl, 'Oh, what a goal'. They don't know what day it is. Don't you worry, when John hits the ball, he means it, and he has a damned good idea of where it's going."

Walter Borthwick loves the way John Robertson will take people on, steaming into the box, challenging, causing . . . yes, panic. "One-to-one, aiming for the goal, he'll do it for you. It's a matter of natural ability, and you can't buy that, not with a private gold-mine."

All Hearts fans will second that proposition. They will also recall the other goal he scored against Dundee United, in that 3-0 win at Tannadice. He had only the goalkeeper to beat—and that's precisely the point. Most professionals will tell you that there are few more demanding situations in the game, for the very good reason that if you win it, success is taken for granted—and, if you lose it, you're a mug. John did the business by virtue of what Walter Borthwick calls natural ability.

He's still just 21, and played for Salvesen Boys Club and Edina Hibs Boys Club before coming to Tynecastle in January 1981. A fairly mixed pedigree, one might suspect. He says he likes lasagne and pineapple and lemonade, which isn't a bad mix either. Like quite a few of his team-mates, his favourite film actor is Clint Eastwood. A pity he didn't take more penalties . . . "All right, you bum in that goal, make my day." He could do a lot worse than Jimmy O'Rourke as a boyhood hero and it is easy to understand why he rates Alex McLeish of Aberdeen as the most difficult opponent he has ever faced. Alex is the most difficult opponent most strikers have ever faced, being distinctly disinclined to permit anybody to go past him under any circumstances.

John Robertson
Hearts v Rangers, 29 March 1986

John Colquhoun has been at Tynecastle for only about a year but it didn't take him nearly as long as that to make an impact. Indeed, it was in his very first game for Hearts that John scored— against Celtic, the club which, for reasons nobody outside Parkhead can understand, let him go.

Alex MacDonald regards him as an exceptional team player, with a formidable work-rate, who will go into the penalty box and cause lots of trouble. "Into the hard places," as some of the more pretentious English football writers love to put it.

But that phrase "work-rate" should not be misunderstood. It was, admittedly, used by Sir Alf Ramsay over and over again in an attempt to cover up his England team's glaring lack of real talent. Alex MacDonald tries no such subterfuge, having no need to do so. "That wee man has great skill," he says. Hearts supporters will certainly not argue, as they recall John Colquhoun's capacity for scoring crucial goals. His ferocious volley, for instance, which took Hearts through the Cup semi-final against Dundee United at Hampden. It wasn't a coincidence that he was in the right spot at the right time. He did have some good games against Hearts when playing for Celtic, a fact that did not go unnoticed by Alex MacDonald. "Well, you know what we do here at Tynecastle," says Alex. "If they play well against us, we go out and buy them."

As an explanation of the Heart of Midlothian recruitment policy, that is possibly an over-simplification, but one can see the manager's point. Celtic and Rangers supporters gabble about their "rejects" at Tynecastle. Some rejects! If they don't know enough in Glasgow to hold on to their most productive players, then whose fault is that?

"John is another player who listens well," says Walter Borthwick. "You can see he is keen on learning. He's also very difficult to knock off the ball."

John achieved one of his ambitions last March, when he met Neil Kinnock who was up for the Scottish Labour Party Conference. The two of them even indulged in some head-tennis, and John thought Neil wasn't too bad at it at all.

For a 22-year-old, he has a few old-fashioned tastes. He

John Colquhoun

insists that his favourite actress is Bette Davis, which explains, partly, why he likes watching old black-and-white films. But he balances that by his choice of reading matter—the *New Musical Express*, which is presumably modern enough.

John Colquhoun was, as we have noted, a very useful player when with Celtic. Since he came to Tynecastle, and since he has been given more freedom to move about, he has improved almost out of all recognition. Another success for the MacDonald-Jardine-Borthwick combination, surely!

Sandy Clark is neither a spectacular nor a glamorous type of player, but nobody—especially none of his team-mates—would ever dream of under-estimating his value to the side. His stamina is phenomenal—at 29, he isn't exactly slowing down—and it needs to be, considering the role he is asked to play. "Sandy takes all the stick, all the thumps, up there in the penalty area," says Walter Borthwick, "and he manages to keep the ball there for the vital fractions of a second until the back-up is there."

"When he goes for the ball," says Sandy Jardine, "everybody knows it. Ask any defender. They all hate playing against him."

Sandy was with West Ham and Airdrie before coming to Hearts. Ah yes, we've missed out Rangers, haven't we? So that makes Sandy Clark yet another reject. If he's any guide, Hearts will take all the rejects they can get. He says he enjoys going back to Ibrox, though, so there can't be any hard feelings . . . unless, perhaps, when Hearts win there, and that is not an especially unusual occurrence.

Alex MacDonald names one of the main reasons why he went for Sandy Clark . . . and it is not the sort of reason normally appreciated by the fans. "I know he's not a prolific scorer of goals," says Alex, "but he is a really intelligent player as well as being so brave. He makes goals for other players not just by bustling a defence, but by thinking. Look at that fine goal Gary Mackay scored against Clydebank, our last match at Tynecastle. The fans saw Gary move one way, swerve the other way, thump the ball into the net. But did they see the way Sandy Clark helped

Sandy Clark runs at the Aberdeen defence
20 April 1986

to draw the defence?"

"You know what is often said about players like Sandy Clark," Sandy Jardine added. "He'll put his head in where others won't put a boot. He's a tremendous asset, and you won't find anybody less conceited, either."

Ian Jardine has a quality which is not given to many. When he is anywhere near the ball, at a free-kick in the other half of the field, he can almost—almost—command a sort of silence. I'm not saying that Tynecastle goes all quiet, and I'm not saying that those who have just come out of the Tynecastle Arms are in respectful mood, but the aura of anticipation is unmistakeable. When Ian hits it, he hits it.

I'm not sure what it means—a source of strength, perhaps—but he reckons that his favourite food is steak, washed down with a couple of pints of milk. Naturally, I can understand very well what he means when he says that he loves reading the *Sunday Mail*—Alan Herron, Don Morrison, Dixon Blackstock, Darlinda—and that is another matter altogether.

It would be very wrong to classify Ian as merely a player who can thump a ball from 30 yards right into the back of the net. Why should I say *merely*? It is not exactly a fault, is it? Lots of us will remember a Scot called Peter Lorimer, who is still very much about the game, and who could scare the living daylights out of most goalkeepers. Older stagers will remember Charlie Fleming of East Fife—"Legs" Fleming. He was in a similar mould.

Alex MacDonald comments about Ian: "He has a lot of courage, and, believe me, in this game that is not to be under-rated. The Premier League doesn't have much scope for cowards. I'll correct that. It doesn't have any scope at all."

"Ian is good under pressure," says Walter Borthwick. "He seems to thrive on it. He makes very few bad passes and he doesn't just shove the ball away for the sake of it. He'll accept responsibility."

Sandy Jardine says: "Ian is a magnificent striker of a ball. Obviously, it's all in the family."

Ian is an Ayrshire lad. He played for Irvine Vics, Kilmarnock

Ian Jardine in action against Rangers
16 November 1985

and Partick Thistle—plus a spell in Cyprus—before signing for Hearts in May 1985.

It is pleasant to know that Ian admires John Greig—pleasant for me, anyway, because I rate big John very highly and that puts me and Ian in a large company. John Greig, after all, has done more for Rangers than all the present directors put together, and, moreover, all of the current players—without exception.

Ian discusses his boss, Alex MacDonald, but, as he does so, he looks back a bit. "He was a hard man to play against. He was *murder* to play against, if you like. You couldn't relax for a moment."

All of which fits in with Alex MacDonald's theory about signing people he really knows all about. Clearly Ian Jardine played better against Alex than he thinks.

We come now to three players who, although not involved as meaningfully as they would have liked in the record-breaking season, have still made a most honourable contribution to the club.

Alex MacDonald makes a special reference to Roddy MacDonald, to Andy Watson and to Billy Mackay. If there were space in this book, he would be talking about more of his lads, and he can only hope that nobody left out will take offence. He doesn't think they will because the harmony within the club is too much cherished for such attitudes as envy, jealousy or pique.

"These lads have been playing in the reserves," says Alex, "and they're always making sure they're one hundred per cent fit. They never stop trying to win a place in the Premier League side. I mean, look at Billy. He was injured and some folk thought he might never play again. He's still in contention all the time and that's why he is a Hearts player. He doesn't give up. That's why they're all Hearts players. Some are in the first team, some are on the fringe, and some are determined to be there, eventually. It's the way we work here, really. We don't have a lot of time for the prima donnas, we do have a good laugh, and we do take things seriously at the right times."

"I've told you before, and I'll tell you again, this is as much a family as it is a club. We work hard, but we also enjoy ourselves. Come on, isn't that what the game is all about? If you don't enjoy playing it, if you don't enjoy being part of it, and never mind about the wages, then you should be doing something else."

Against all odds for Clark and MacDonald at Dens Park
3 May 1986

*Scotland's top two managers, Alex Ferguson and Alex MacDonald
lead out their Cup Final teams*

The Inner Sanctum

Pilmar Smith, the Hearts director for whom Tynecastle Park seems a kind of second home, told me, without hesitation, that if I wanted to know anything about the inner workings of the club, then I should waste no time in having a talk with Les Porteous, the secretary. Pilmar, an ebullient and tremendously shrewd little man, knew, as usual, what he was talking about.

Les occupies the office behind one of the best-known parts of Tynecastle . . . the wee window-hatch where the fans press a button and ask for tickets. His assistant, Yvonne, demure and quietly efficient, handles most of the enquiries from the public during the week. Les sits in the middle of the nerve-centre although, to be very honest, a first impression might interpret that as a slightly pretentious description. It reminds me of a newspaper office. It is a guddle. Les wouldn't deny as much. And yet, again perhaps like a newspaper office, things work well.

In no way at all does it resemble the average secretary's office at a big football club. At so many such clubs, the atmosphere is, not to mince words, stand-offish. No doubt there are exceptions. But the rule seems clear: we only want to see you people on match days, when you pay plenty for the privilege. Otherwise, leave us alone.

Indeed, few would question that that was how Tynecastle itself used to be. One must be fair. But the change has been dramatic—and the change took place moments after Les Porteous walked in the door six years ago. All formalities, all pomposities, were swept away. On the outside of the office door, true, there is the sign, "Secretary". But you don't bother to knock when you enter. You poke your head in, ask for Les, and that's the ceremony over.

Maybe that partly explains why the office is, well, somewhat untidy. Photographs of incidents from Hearts matches more or less cover one wall—alongside a chart detailing the conduct record of each individual player. That certainly isn't for decoration. Jerseys, boots, old and new footballs lie scattered around among various trophies and mementoes—none of them, admittedly, especially recent. On one sideboard, there's a concession to secretarial matters—a typewriter. And, of course, the telephones, which would have been red-hot these past few weeks if they hadn't been plastic.

Viewing all this, what might an expert in time and motion think, apart, that is, from expecting to see Les Porteous running round the walls without touching the floor? That is what he might have felt like at times. If so, it certainly wasn't obvious. The man is unflappable.

Yvonne calls through to say that there's a couple of electricians walking in as if they owned the place, and is this really all right? Les clears it all up with a weary smile and an assurance. Yvonne nods and gets back to explaining to a customer why he can't really have the Cup Final seats he wants.

Sandy Jardine comes in. He's about to be off training and he spends a few minutes exercising in front of the electric fire. The kind of exercises you see from substitutes during a game. Bending and turning and generally creaking every conceivable muscle apart from the eyelids. "Well," says Sandy, "it's the old bones, isn't it? The rest of them, they limber up outside. It's all right for them."

For a moment, one suspects he's looking for sympathy, but for only a moment. One remembers how he controlled the defence the previous Saturday, old bones or no old bones.

The door bursts open and Wallace Mercer brings in a couple

A maiden marooned ... with plenty of company from Berry, Mackay, Levein and Colquhoun

of Swedish journalists. He asks them if they'd like a cup of coffee—one each, reasonably enough—and they decline. They just want to talk about Hearts and they have heard and seen so much of Henry Smith. Here is another example of the Tynecastle open-door policy. The Swedes hadn't made an appointment. They had just turned up, hoping for the best. They were welcomed.

Wallace has a quick chat with Les. He deals with some correspondence. "That one, that's an invitation to play in Nigeria. We can't make it, not yet."

In mid-April, that doesn't seem too impolite.

"And that's somebody wanting to build a new grandstand for us," says Wallace. "I reckon we can leave that out for the time being. Never mind, who can tell for the future?"

He smiles widely.

Craig Levein has a query for Les Porteous, and he also has five horses for that day. Craig has a contact in the racing game, it seems, and he is also quite optimistic. He's trying to explain all this when Sandy Jardine, finished shaking those ancient bones in his limbering up by now, shouts through from the corridor.

"Any time you're ready, Craig."

This courtesy has a not-so-gentle hint of irony. Craig takes no offence whatsoever. He gets off his mark. Incidentally, his horses don't win. At least one had no chance at all. Two were in the same race.

Willie Montgomery, the groundsman, has heard that there's a damp stain on the wall above Les Porteous's desk. He comes in and has a look. "I'm worried in case it's that toilet upstairs," he says.

By this time, Les has coped with everything from long-lost mates seeking Cup Final tickets to the possibility of a leaky toilet right above his head. He remains unflappable. He wears a jersey, originated by Pringle, but with his name emblazoned on the right breast. He may not be as modest as he pretends to be. But modesty is for those who have good reason for modesty. I can see no reason why Les Porteous should be concerned by such a doubtful virtue. He knows his job too well for that. He is 38-years-old, and that is, presumably, a long way from senility. He has friends—friends?—who insist that if he stays secretary of the Hearts, he will achieve premature senility. Clearly they do not support the Heart of Midlothian Football Club.

For Les Porteous, the secretaryship of the club is not so much a privilege as a labour of love. It doesn't have much to do with the daily grind of earning a living—although, in rent-book or mortgage-society terms, that is precisely what it is. The main point is that Les Porteous loves the club, and, as we have noted elsewhere in this book, this counts for a very great deal. His grandfather played for Hearts in the early part of this century, and—his name was Bill—he won a Scottish Cup medal. "My blood is coloured maroon," Les says, without seeking an argument. "It's a family thing. It is handed down. You've not got much choice, have you?"

He looks around at the pictures of the season, pictures showing Colquhoun, Robertson and just about every other

Levein rises over Leighton in a league match

Hearts player. "It's important," he says, "that they know, I mean *know* that they can come in and see me any time they like."

On top of one of the filing cabinets, there's a cheap football, one of the £7 versions autographed by the players, and there's also a box with the label, "Trivial Pursuits".

"The lads love that game," says Les. "Or, anyway, some of them do. They all want a go. They hate it if they're wrong. Yes, certainly, they fall out, but not for long. You must hear this all over the club—we're talking about a family. The spirit of competition is essential here and on the park."

Les arrived at Tynecastle just as Willie Ormond was leaving. He didn't have time to know Willie and he appreciates that this was unfortunate. He reckons that they would have got along very well. I would think that this is true. Willie was a man quite without what is called "side", and he could get along with anybody. So can Les. He comes from Newtongrange, which is possibly the next best thing to coming from Gorebridge. (At this point, I would like to believe that readers who happen to have been brought up in different places will excuse my confessed lack of neutrality. We cannot all claim to have been born in Gorgie Road or McLeod Street, overlooking the ground. Also, at this point, my own antecedents go back to Birkenside, where I could look at, and listen to, the Fushiebridge Pipe Band on a Saturday night. Certainly, all this is nostalgia. So what on earth is wrong with that? Without nostalgia, where is the tradition? Without tradition, where is the love of a club?)

And so Les Porteous comes from Newtongrange, where he still lives a few doors from where he was brought up, and where Dave Mackay played junior football. Les commutes each day and, to his credit, has never even considered moving in closer to, say, The Grange, Morningside, or Constitution Street. Well, why should he?

As they say as often as they can in the Dean Tavern, under the supervision of the excellent Mr Yuill, it's God's own country. Personally speaking, I would say that it is close. Less than a couple of miles away, up in the braes, is Arniston and, more importantly, Arniston Rangers, where Bobby Kirk comes from, and for whom he played. THAT is where the deity comes from But we digress. All I'm trying to say, really, is that Les Porteous is one of us, and always will be.

He was educated at Dalkeith High, an establishment not known for its willingness to tolerate idiots—listen, believe me, I know—and served for a while in the time office at the old Lady Victoria pit. Younger readers should note that the Lady Vic, usually known as "The Lady", is now transformed into a mining museum. Should you wish to look around this museum, I am sure Les will give you a guided tour and then again, he may not. He was less than happy there, as he was during his whole term with the Coal Board. And they hadn't heard of Mr McGregor then. "No," he says. "It's just that a lot of them above me didn't know any more than me."

That could be an attitude liable to strike a sympathetic chord with very many of us, but we'll leave it out for now.

Les served briefly under Bobby Moncur and Tony Ford. The

Colquhoun jumps—Levein and Robertson watch anxiously, at Hampden

Sandy Clark in a typical joust during the Cup Final

brevity of such service was hardly anything to do with him. That era he is not inclined to elaborate on, and I can't blame him. I knew Bobby Moncur as a player—and he was a very good player, at both club and at international level. But he always wanted to do everything by himself. He seemed inherently incapable of delegating responsibility. In other words, he was more of an administrator than a manager—IF you concede, and I think you should, that the term "manager" nowadays really means coach. AND boss.

Tony Ford didn't last very long, a few months, and although he was a pleasant enough lad, he had little chance of lasting long. He did tend to adopt the theory that if anything went wrong, it could be put right by more hours of training. This is not something likely to attract a lot of comment from Les Porteous. He is not only efficient, he is also a born diplomat. (Even when directors telephone him about tickets, and I mean scarce tickets, he has a charming way of telling them that it's not quite as simple as that.)

He is far more forthcoming when discussing the new and incomparably more successful régime at Tynecastle. But you won't find him sycophantic to anybody. This is doubtless a tribute to his upbringing. In mining villages, sycophants are thin on the ground. They are then, of course, stamped on.

He has a lot of time for Wallace Mercer, but he points out that he knows how Wallace is likely to react to any given situation. If that makes Les Porteous rather more than the accepted idea of a secretary, I won't argue. For the mutual respect between Wallace and Les is clear. And Les has his own theories about how Hearts did so well in season 1985-86. Incidentally, he is at least as entitled as anybody to have such theories. Possibly a lot more than most.

I thought we'd be in the first five," he says, "because we were playing well enough for that. Alex was working so hard, and so was Sandy, and they were picking the right teams, they were getting the tactics right. Mr Mercer was projecting the image of the club, the other directors were involved, especially Pilmar, and, honestly, something *had* to happen."

"Of course, and let's never forget this, Alex and Sandy were the boys. A lot of weeding out was done. I rate Alex very, very highly—not only as a football manager but as a man. You can't say that about every manager can you, not if you're being honest?"

"I like to think I back up the board and management. What I never do is make any big decision without the involvement of the chairman or the manager, but we're still very much a team, a family. There's a lot of trust. There has to be. Nobody lets anybody down."

Les Porteous subscribes very strongly, then, to the whole atmosphere of togetherness at Tynecastle, and believes warmly that this is a cogent factor in the emergence of Hearts as one of the most formidable forces in Scottish football.

"The manager has so much to do with this," he says. "So far as I know, he has never taken a degree in psychology or even something in man-management, but, as far as I'm concerned, he shouldn't be a pupil, he should be a tutor. He has this gift for getting folk to do exactly as he says, even if they don't agree with him. Sometimes I worry that he is so underrated, and I'm telling you, he IS underrated. That's some team, Alex and Sandy."

"But you know, I've seen Alex stop a young player in the corridor, and birl him round, and show him where he had gone wrong with some specific move in the last match. He'll say, this is where you went wrong, and he'll say, this is what you do to put it right. Everybody listens to him, and to Sandy, because these two have been there, they've been at the very top and they know what they're talking about."

"Once, there was this player with a good reputation in England. He came up here on a free transfer and he was looking for a place at Tynecastle. A lot of the players knew about him and they were talking about him. You know, they were a wee bit over-awed. I mean, he wasn't that old, far from it. Well, the manager heard him talking about this and that, like a couple of pints when you couldn't sleep, to the younger players, and the next day, in comes the manager: 'Les,' he says, 'what's his expenses? Let him go!'"

Wallace Mercer has always believed in following a good example, and improving on it. Before coming to Hearts he had noted how, on the Continent, the big clubs were administratively split in two. One department for the football club itself. The other for outside income, sponsors and the like.

It made so much sense.

And that's why Les Porteous handles the administration connected with the football . . . with Robin Fry in charge of the commercial aspects.

Robin, a former professional footballer with Bristol City, Swindon and Bournemouth, divides his time between the commercial premises at Tynecastle and the rather grander office on the ninth floor of a block dominating the Mound, overlooking Princes Street.

Still only 33, he positively crackles with energy. It is easy enough to see why he and Wallace Mercer hit it off almost immediately. "Mind you," he says, "Wallace is a hard task-master. He doesn't hesitate to kick backsides. Often. He's not a man you can blind with science, that's for sure."

From the commercial department of the Hearts, substantial financial blessings flow. Robin reckons he is on target for a £200,000 net profit—"and I do mean net"—this year. That goes to the football club. "It helps Alex MacDonald to have an 18-strong pool," Robin says, "and I suppose it also helps with bonuses. But that's not my concern. My job is to sell the club's image as hard and as aggressively as I can."

He doesn't have much time for clubs which lack sponsorship and which blame this on ordinary team results. "That's just an excuse," he says. "We've been succcessfully selling to sponsors for the last three seasons. A winning team is an added extra, but greatly appreciated. It certainly makes my job a little easier. Now

August 1985
Hearts go Japanese in finding a new sponsor

potential sponsors phone us, rather than the other way round."

One can see what he means. Already 80 per cent of the main match sponsorship has been sold for next season. And that's before the fixture list is known. "People call," Robin says, "and ask for the first game against, say, Rangers or Hibs. They may not get it. Depends on availability. But it's encouraging to have such a strong demand."

Obviously, business firms more or less monopolise the main weekly sponsorship. If the visiting side is Rangers, Celtic, Hibs or Aberdeen that sponsorship will cost about £5,000. The scale descends to £2,000. And what do they get for their money? VIP treatment—what else? A party of up to 22 is ferried from a central point to the ground, where there's a four-course lunch, lavish refreshments, hostesses and, generally, everything except a guaranteed result for the team of one's choice. The treatment continues at half-time and after the game. Programme and board advertising is included as is, of course, comfortable seating in the glass-fronted sponsorship lounge.

Then there are secondary sponsors. A party of 20—transport, food, drink, box seats—is well looked after, for up to £1,500. The weekly match-ball sponsor pays £250 for four people, and that includes the advertising, seats and entertaining facilities with drinks and savouries laid on. You can, of course, sponsor a player for the season. That costs £100 and you get your name in the programme.

"We're all for the package deals," says Robin. "And we like to do everything in style. The office at the Mound is important. It's where we discuss deals in elegant surroundings. I'm not apologising for it . . . image matters."

Sponsorship apart, his department takes care of most travel arrangements, lotteries and big-match tickets. He remembers with justifiable pride how he organised travel and hotels for 4,000 fans when Hearts played in Paris a couple of years ago. "And, naturally, we did the special charter plane for the team and the Executive Club."

When he talks about the Executive Club, he does so with an unmistakeable gratitude. This is the club with its own premises

Pictured at Tynecastle are manager Alex MacDonald (right)
and assistant manager/player Sandy Jardine (left)

next to the boardroom. It has about 50 members now, all fairly
well-heeled members of the populace. "But do you know what I
did, when I wanted to build the new sponsorship lounge?" Robin
asks. "Remember our projects have to be self-funding. Well, I
went to the Exec Club, and asked for four years' subscription up
front. In no time at all I had forty grand, which was what I
needed. The club subscriptions have also helped to build the
players' lounge."

Hearts plan to build a new restaurant at Tynecastle soon. It
will cost £20,000, but will be sponsored by Alloa Brewery. "Again
self-funding," says Robin. "Like the record of *The Hearts Song* ...
that was underwritten by Marshall's Chunky Chicken."

After leaving pro football—and he was good at the
game—Robin moved into coaching with Hereford and then into
promotions and consultancy. It was as a consultant that he made

his first contact with Hearts, when Archie Martin was chairman.

He admits that in England he had to handle short-sighted directors, the Establishment types who still lived in the days of baggy pants and boots like boats. "It was as if they didn't really want to be bothered with bringing more money in. They were so out-of-date, I lived in a state of continuous frustration."

He's not frustrated now. With Wallace Mercer around, he hasn't the time to be!

Kenny Black rises to the occasion at Hampden

Match by Match

THOSE WHO FOLLOW the Heart of Midlothian Football Club are dedicated optimists. They have little choice. Over the past century or so, they have been sustained rather more by hope than by trophies and titles. Indeed it is a long-established joke to ask at the start of a new season: Will this be Hearts' year? Everybody answers "Yes", in chorus.

The question was asked, as usual, in August 1985. Answers in the affirmative were no more serious than they had ever been in the past. There was that traditional hope. But most fans would have been happy to be guaranteed a place in the top half of the League and, perhaps, with lots of luck, one of the European minor places. The bookmakers, picking numbers out of their heads, quite sure that it was academic anyway, were laying up to 150-1 against Hearts for the title.

And yet—maybe with slight benefit of hindsight—optimism might have been more in order than for some time. The final league placing for 1984-85 didn't seem particularly promising— fourth from the bottom—but there had been strong hints of better things to come from a playing pool spiced by hard experience and blossoming young talent. The chairman had made it plain that no effort would be spared to keep stars like John Robertson, Craig Levein, Kenny Black and Gary Mackay. We now know that the promise was kept. Before the season even started, a £200,000 offer for Craig Levein from another unnamed Premier League club was firmly rejected. And Hearts signed John Colquhoun and Ian Jardine. These signings did not cause a great stir at the time, but Alex MacDonald and Sandy Jardine knew what they were doing. It took no time at all for Colquhoun to establish himself as a favourite at Tynecastle. Well, to be more exact, it took him 28 minutes.

Hearts 1 Celtic 1
10 August 1985

Walter Kidd, Kenny Black and Roddy MacDonald, not too well behaved the previous season, missed this glamorous opening match through suspension. But Neil Berry was back after injury.

And let there be no doubt . . . Celtic took a point home to Glasgow only by virtue of great good fortune. They had beaten Hearts four times in 1984-85, but they never looked like continuing that record into the new season. Their forwards showed little bite against a Hearts defence in almost constant control, although it must be admitted that the game, as a whole, was notable for frantic effort rather than for elegant skills.

At least one exception to that rule, however, was wee John Colquhoun in his debut. As so often happens in similar circumstances, John relished the chance to indicate that Celtic had been unwise to let him go—even for £50,000. With Celtic, he had been confined to the left-wing. Now he was weaving and dribbling more or less where he pleased and the Celtic defenders didn't like it. They liked it even less when, from a John Robertson corner, Colquhoun scored smartly. Time: 28 minutes. He could have had two more goals before half-time, and Robertson was a little unlucky too.

As the match progressed, that single goal looked increasingly liable to be enough for Hearts. The trouble was that Celtic, like Rangers, had a reputation for battling to the end . . . a reputation they were determined to keep. And so, in the final minute, Paul McStay equalised. An injury to Berry with six minutes left hadn't helped, but it was not an excuse.

Colquhoun in action with Danny McGrain

Hearts:	Smith: Berry, Cherry (sub 84 mins), Jardine, Levein, Whittaker, Sandison, Watson, Mackay, Colquhoun, Clark, Robertson.
Celtic:	Bonner: W. McStay, Aitken, McAdam, Burns, Grant, P. McStay, Macleod, Provan, Johnston, McClair, McInally (sub 72 mins).
Referee:	H. Alexander, Kilmarnock.

The following Tuesday 13 August, a crowd of about 7,500 turned up at Tynecastle to see an Edinburgh Select versus Bayern Munich in a challenge match labelled as for the Festival Trophy. The Edinburgh side won 2-1 and John Robertson again emphasised his precocious talent by scoring one of the goals, creating the other for Willie Irvine and generally giving the German defence a most difficult evening.

The *Scotsman* said the next morning that the match might have helped to fashion friendlier relations between the Hearts and Hibs fans, but with such a tiny crowd that seemed an over-optimistic viewpoint. I'm afraid—if that's the right word—that the alternative theory was more likely to be true. Hearts fans will turn up to watch Hearts and Hibs fans will turn up to watch Hibs, but they're not too keen on a mixture.

St. Mirren 6 Hearts 2
17 August 1985

I don't think we need spend a lot of time on this one, do you? It was Hearts' worst defeat since the MacDonald-Jardine managerial partnership was established. After that excellent performance against Celtic, the substantial travelling support emerged from Love Street somewhat shell-shocked, baffled as to how Hearts could have made so many mistakes, notably in defence.

Even Sandy Jardine seemed nervous and, on occasion, downright careless. Yet Hearts scored first, through Colquhoun in the 14th minute. We can only speculate now on what might have happened had John Robertson taken an easy chance in the very first minute. Idle speculation indeed! Robertson did score

Brian Whittaker, against St Mirren

eventually, but by that time St Mirren had knocked in six and it didn't matter very much.

But as this is being written nine months after the event, we can certainly look back and reflect on how much St Mirren have affected Hearts. The defeat and the six goals counted formidably in the final analysis. It's no good wishing, however, that St Mirren had produced this form against Celtic on the *last* day of the season. They weren't that good. Hearts happened to be awful.

St Mirren:	Money: Wilson, Hamilton, Rooney, Godfrey, Clarke, Fitzpatrick, Mackie, McGarvie, Gallacher, Speirs.
Hearts:	Smith: Sandison, Whittaker, Jardine, MacDonald, Levein, Colquhoun, Watson, Clark, Robertson, Mackay.
Referee:	A. Ferguson, Giffnock.

On the following Tuesday there was more cheerful intelligence to report. Hearts went up to Montrose and reached the third round of the Skol League Cup. But it wasn't easy, and there were those who remembered how Montrose had given Hearts a sore time of it in the 1976 Scottish Cup quarter-final—Hearts winning then 3-2, only after extra-time, at Muirton.

It was not the kind of history one would have wanted to see repeated. Montrose had won the Second Division championship the previous season and were determined not to be treated lightly. In this, they succeeded. Not until well into the second-half, when a Colquhoun shot was deflected into the net by a defender, was there any reason for Hearts to feel reasonably relaxed. The other Hearts goals in a 3-1 win, were scored by Kidd (a freakish 30-yarder) and by Robertson.

The draw for the third round matched Hearts against Stirling, and it was known simultaneously that the winners would meet St Johnstone or Aberdeen away from home in the fourth round. This, as many fans will remember, led to some friction between Hearts and Aberdeen over ticket allocations for the obviously likely tie at Pittodrie. It was all sorted out in the end. These things usually are. But I suppose Wallace Mercer was really trying to avoid a repetition of the chaos of the previous season when many Hearts fans were locked out of Pittodrie at a Scottish Cup-tie.

Rangers 3 Hearts 1
24 August 1985

Now here we had a somewhat unfortunate occasion, in more ways than one. In the *Sunday Mail* the highly perceptive Don Morrison called it a superb exhibition of unarmed combat. He went rather further than that. "With three players ordered off and eight booked," said our Don, "it was just the stuff to give Ernie Walker and his clean-up-the-game brigade apoplexy."

This summing-up appeared to be fair enough to all who were there. The game provided little evidence in support of the theory that Hearts and Rangers were busy trying to carve up Scottish

Colquhoun comes close against Rangers

football . . . we refer, naturally, to the number of so-called Rangers rejects mentioned elsewhere in this book. If Rangers were willing to be nice to Hearts on this occasion, you could have fooled 35,483 paying customers.

Poor Douglas Hope, who had drawn the short straw, and who was therefore condemned to be the referee (he couldn't have known what would happen, otherwise he would surely have had 'flu), must have been concerned about whether he had enough red and yellow cards in his pocket.

That, ladies and gentlemen, is a joke. We all know perfectly well that a referee doesn't actually give the cards away. One of each colour is enough. Even so, Mr Hope had a hard time.

Football, as the *Evening News* said, took second place. Well, that was also fair comment. At that particular moment, the film *Rambo* had not gone on general view, which was just as well. It gave President Reagan dangerous ideas. Hearts and Rangers needed no such inspiration.

71

There was some football played. Not a lot. But the ration had a certain quality of excitement anyway. Rangers took an early enough grip in the middle of the park and Davie Cooper looked good. We Hearts supporters must confess . . . this lad Cooper can play the game! He has class. The late Jock Stein was at the match. How tragic that Jock wasn't permitted the time to exploit fully the fine talent of Cooper.

But Mr Hope was never able to relax. Certainly no referee should ever be allowed to relax, but you know what I mean. He booked big Sandy Clark, who was presumably intent on making sure that his old club knew he was there. That was in the 20th minute, or near enough.

Ally McCoist caused embarrassment to Hearts. He could easily have scored, but made a mess of it. John Robertson was cautioned for a challenge on the Rangers goalkeeper, a challenge owing more to John's enthusiasm than to any chance of actually getting the ball into the net. Never mind, John made up for that a few minutes before half-time.

Dave McPherson took an unorthodox view of the rules, as John burst through, clear. From the free-kick, John scored from the edge of the box, almost certainly by courtesy of a deflection. It was hardly noticed when Durrant was cautioned for a foul on Wattie Kidd just on half-time.

The real problems started in the second-half, when Rangers went like the clappers, as they say, for an equalising goal. Kidd, emphasising in a way the determination of Hearts to stay ahead, was cautioned.

Hugh Burns elbowed and prodded his way past Hearts to score, and Williamson got the other goals that won the game. The referee was possibly too lenient in the way he overlooked Burns' provocative reaction to the crowd. But he (Burns) is only a teenager, and his exuberance may be forgiven.

Much more difficult to excuse though was the nonsense later on. Larry Holmes might have been at home. Mohammed Ali, being a sophisticated and essentially graceful man, might have been struggling. Enough to say that Kidd appeared not to miss Bell and that McCoist and Clark decided this might be a good time to go boxing. Messrs Kidd, Clark and McCoist were all told that they would have no further interest in the proceedings, by Mr Hope, who did as efficient a job as might have been expected in the circumstances.

So these were two more points lost, and to a team later proved to be much inferior to Hearts. In fact, they were no better on that day itself. But a championship is all about consistency of quality. Hearts were still not making the case firmly enough.

Rangers:	Walker: Burns, Munro, McPherson, Paterson, Bell, McCoist, Russell, Williamson, Durrant, Cooper.
Hearts:	Smith: Kidd, Whittaker, Jardine, R. MacDonald, Levein, Colquhoun, Watson, Clark, Cowie, Robertson.
Referee:	D. Hope, Erskine.

There was an unhappy, if not unexpected, aftermath to that Ibrox performance. It had been worse than the ordering-off of three players. Too many others had been more than willing to

Keeper's ball

join in. Nobody in the press box—and very few anywhere else at Ibrox—doubted that such mayhem off the park would inevitably have resulted in appearances at the Sheriff Court.

There were some aspects worthy of consolation. The crowd was remarkably well behaved. And TV wasn't there. That last point is not a small one. After the slaughter in Brussels at the European Cup Final, football didn't need any wider projection of what happened at Ibrox.

A few days later, Hearts moved on to the Skol League Cup, but they had many a worried moment before managing to get the better of Stirling Albion. It needed extra-time for their 2-1 win.

All Hearts fans who were there will recall how they felt—unless they've had worse memories intruding since, of course—when Stirling were leading with only 16 minutes left. And this at Tynecastle! That was when Brian McNaughton scored. And it was Paul Cherry who headed in a Robertson cross in the 101st minute.

Full-time training probably told in the end. But for far too long Stirling Albion seemed likely to make nonsense of any Hearts' complaint about tickets at Aberdeen for the next round. Meanwhile, Sandy Jardine was watching Hibs score six against Motherwell. The prospects for the big Edinburgh derby didn't seem too inviting.

Hearts 2 Hibs 1
31 August 1985

Ironically, in view, what was to happen some months later, and on an even more important occasion, there was talk of a "mystery virus" at Tynecastle the day before the local derby. But nobody took much notice: it is almost tradition that neither club likes to reveal its selection in advance. In fact, it's not so much a tradition as a ritual. As it happened, only Brian Whittaker was left out of the Hearts team, because of illness, and it was being more and more appreciated that George Cowie could play well just about anywhere.

John Robertson

It was a terrible match.

I remember being quite unable to raise any real enthusiasm for Sandy Clark's winner eight minutes from time. It was a good enough goal, earned by the tenacity of Clark as he punished a mistake by Rae. But, as one considered the appalling stuff that had wasted the previous 82 minutes, it didn't seem worthwhile making any cracks to Hibbie friends.

However, it must be conceded that if anybody deserved to win, a doubtful proposition, then Hearts just about came into that category. They produced most of the aggression, thanks mainly to Robertson and Colquhoun. And it was Colquhoun who was credited with the opening goal, although the other John had done most of the work. One consolation taken from the game—victory apart—was the blossoming, increasingly menacing talents of the two little men.

Durie, whose own tenacity matched that of Clark, equalised after about half-an-hour, but as early as this eyes were becoming glazed with boredom. I had always believed that by virtue of the occasion itself, a Hearts-Hibs match could never be boring. This one proved me wrong. Luckily, there was so much better to come, wasn't there? I only wish I'd suspected as much at the time.

Hearts:	Smith: Kidd, Levein, Jardine, MacDonald, Cowie, Watson, Mackay (sub 59 mins), Black, Colquhoun, Clark, Robertson.
Hibs:	Rough: Sneddon, Hunter, Fulton, Munro, Durie, Weir, Brazil, Harris, Kane, Rae (sub 4 mins), Cowan.
Referee:	B. McGinlay, Balfron.

Meanwhile, relations between Hearts and Aberdeen were not yet as friendly as they might have been. By a coincidence that was not welcomed, the two clubs were due to meet twice within the space of a few days. On the Wednesday, there was the Skol League Cup fourth-round tie, and, of course, the scheduled Premier League match on the Saturday.

With some justification, Wallace Mercer was displeased by an offer of only 400 tickets from Aberdeen for the cup-tie and even more displeased on hearing that the Grampian police had insisted on this tiny allocation. And so Hearts fans were strongly advised not to travel. "I must stress," said the Tynecastle chairman, however, "that there is no personal vendetta against either Aberdeen or the Scottish League. I am merely airing my club's views."

Another wrangle was continuing simultaneously, with Sandy Clark and Walter Kidd asking the Court of Session to rule against a three-match ban. It will be remembered that the players received an automatic one-match ban for incidents in the match at Ibrox—then were banned for three more because of "the exceptional nature of the incident". But Lord Mayfield, giving judgement, said he could not form a view as to whether it was all against natural justice and refused an interdict.

It was not, then, the best of backgrounds in which to face two obviously demanding games. The cup-tie scoreline was respectable enough, though ... 1-0 for Aberdeen. For that, Henry Smith deserved much credit. There would be no point in suggesting that Hearts were, in any way, unfortunate. On that day, Aberdeen proved demonstrably superior. And so on to the league game.

Aberdeen 3 Hearts 0
7 September 1985

The first week in September—and if the bookies had been offering 150-1 for the title earlier in the season, they were now being severely criticised for being so miserable. Curiously, however, Hearts played considerably better in this match than they had in the League Cup-tie. This, mind you, despite the almost complete absence of Hearts' supporters, who had been banned from travelling north. Alex MacDonald commented colourfully: "Having no fans in the crowd is not a healthy position. It's just like the Christians facing the Romans in the Colosseum without having anybody to cheer them on."

Bett you don't!
Kenny Black against Aberdeen in a league match

But as we have noted, Hearts put up rather harder opposition than the Christians are supposed to have done. For the first half-hour, indeed, Hearts looked like the team permitted swords. They were certainly faster than the Dons, and a lot nippier. That burly Aberdeen defence must have been wondering what was going on. Such treatment was not at all something to which they were accustomed. Not for a long time had Willie Miller and Alex McLeish been given such a runaround. They seemed like cart-horses against the darting raids of Colquhoun, McNaughton and Cherry. But what Hearts didn't do was score goals, although creating at least three fine chances in an early 15-minute spell. It was a surprise when Billy Stark headed in a corner-kick in the 32nd minute, but that was no consolation to Hearts. We did see signs of the impressive fighting spirit that was to matter so much later on, but Aberdeen had all of the luck as well as all of the goals. And their chances were expertly, even spectacularly, taken by Wright and Black.

Aberdeen:	Leighton: McKimmie, Mitchell, Stark, Wright (sub 71 mins), McLeish, Miller, Black, Simpson, McDougall, Cooper (sub 55 mins), Bett, Hewitt.
Hearts:	Smith: Cowie, Whittaker, Jardine, R. MacDonald, Levein, Colquhoun, Mackay (sub 81 mins), Watson, McNaughton, Cherry, Black, Sandison (sub 83 mins).
Referee:	M. Delaney, Cleland.

Clearly, the Hearts Premier League side was by no means a settled one yet, but that was no fault of Alex MacDonald or of Sandy Jardine. The chief problem was one, quite simply, of injuries. As Hearts planned for the home game against Dundee United there were doubts about both Kenny Black and John Robertson, who had missed the Pittodrie game with a thigh strain. Another problem, which could hardly be put down to bad luck was, of course, suspensions. Sandy Clark and Walter Kidd were still serving their sentences. But there was confidence around Tynecastle all the same for the United confrontation. Possibly because they hadn't so far been beaten at home. No great feat, but at least the confidence wasn't misplaced . . .

Sandy Jardine heads clear from Davie Dodds

Hearts 2 Dundee United 0
14 September 1985

This was the match which assured Hearts fans, yet again, that Neil Berry, recruited on a "free" from Bolton, was going to be a formidable asset. The assessment certainly hasn't been proved wrong since, has it?

79

And the two points taken from a club established as one of the current "Big Four" were absolutely crucial. Before the match Hearts had only three points—one more than Motherwell, three more than Hibs. There was a danger of being left behind. That sounds daft, looking back. It was only too true then.

Here's another daft statistic, and still quite accurate even so. Hearts against Dundee United and only 7,600 bother to watch! They stood in unbroken silence for a minute, a tribute to the memory of Jock Stein, whose tragic and untimely death in Cardiff had saddened the entire world of football.

Two minutes later, they were cheering their heads off.

That was when John Colquhoun swung over a precisely placed corner-kick . . . precisely placed, that is, to the forehead of big Roddy MacDonald. We all know how dangerous Roddy can be at a corner-kick, even when tightly marked. This time he wasn't marked at all and McAlpine, in the United goal, might as well have been a statue. One can only guess at what Jim McLean, not an especially tolerant individual at the best of times, was saying about his defence.

There are few more pleasant boosts to morale than a quick goal and Hearts, although re-shuffled substantially, made the most of it. The defence was beautifully organised, another hint of future successes, and they seemed to have a lot more resolution than United.

The quality of the Tannadice men was not to be doubted. How could it be with such names as Malpas, Gough, Narey, Bannon, Sturrock, Dodds? But they were too concerned about looking pretty, one felt. They wanted to string passes together, which is all very well but not when there's a tendency to stand back and admire one's work.

Hearts didn't stand back. They absorbed the United pressure without too much trouble and were always likely to break fast and dangerously. And it was a Colquhoun corner, touched on by Cowie, that let John Robertson put Hearts two up.

Hearts: Smith: Cowie, Whittaker, S. Jardine, MacDonald, Levein, Colquhoun, Watson, McNaughton, Robertson (sub 54 mins), Berry, Cherry.

Dundee United: McAlpine: Malpas, Kirkwood, Gough, Hegarty, Narey, Bannon, Milne, Clark (sub 66 mins), Redford, Beedie (sub 54 mins), Sturrock, Dodds.

Referee: J. Renton, Cowdenbeath.

Motherwell 2 Hearts 1
21 September 1985

Another away defeat and, despite flashes of real promise at home, it was still a struggle to maintain any kind of safety net in the Premier League. Yes, everybody was talking, then, about safety. A negative attitude, possibly, but an understandable one.

So those two points lost at Fir Park provided genuine cause for anxiety. They put Motherwell on the four-point mark with seven games played, only one point behind Hearts who had played a similar number. Hibs, whose game against Clydebank was postponed, still had no points at all. Rangers led with eleven, one above Celtic. Of course these were early days but it was

A sturdy tackle on John Colquhoun in the Motherwell match

obvious that Hearts would have to start winning, or at least not losing, away from home.

Not that they were all that bad at Fir Park and it has to be remembered that they were under-strength. But Alex MacDonald was surely still entitled to be puzzled by the slack defending—such a dramatic difference from the previous week. One headline said of the Fir Park defeat: "Struggling Hearts Blunder On". It was not, I'm afraid, a grotesque distortion of the facts . . .

Of course it was good to see Ian Jardine score his first goal for Hearts. Ian was a substitute and he took the chance well. He had been on the park for no more than a minute when he exploited a defensive error.

Unfortunately, there was a bit more to it than that. Hearts should have been comfortably ahead by the 25-minute mark. Motherwell defended as if they had no intention of giving anything away at all, and they had to be respected for that. But when the home midfield men started to make an impact, one could almost prophesy the demise of Hearts.

By the way, this was the game of the bomb-scare, only one of two scares of its kind during the whole season in Scotland. Or in Britain. The half-time interval was extended by at least 20 minutes, while fans were asked to evacuate the covered enclosure opposite the stand. The terracing was searched. At the time the score was 0-0, so all of the predictable jokes about the evil intentions of the Edinburgh supporters fell rather flat.

The teams came back and the goals flew in. Two in three minutes, no less. Ian Jardine got his, but what happened then to the Hearts defence? Even Henry Smith made a mess of it and Andy Harrow had no trouble in scoring against us. The mistakes, frankly, were elementary. John Gahagan got the winner in the 55th minute when he found himself with a chance from a mere 12 yards out.

Hearts might have had a penalty when Forbes brought down Robertson with a tackle that owed nothing whatsoever to the recognised laws of the game, but that can be nothing more than a useless recrimination.

After Fir Park, we were saying to ourselves that if Hearts couldn't win there, then they couldn't win anywhere. We did not, you understand, have the gift of second sight.

Motherwell: Gardiner: Dornan, Forbes, McCart, Wishart, Blair, Clark (sub 88 mins), Doyle, Wright, Gahagan, Reilly, Harrow.

Hearts: Smith: Cowie, S. Jardine, MacDonald, I. Jardine (sub 40 mins), Levein, Watson, McNaughton (sub 70 mins), Berry, Whittaker, Colquhoun, Robertson, Cherry.

Referee: R. Valentine, Dundee.

Colin McAdam was now at Tynecastle. He had come back home from Australia, about 8lb over his fighting weight, but full of enthusiasm. He had played in a reserve game against Motherwell and Sandy Jardine reckoned he needed about a couple of weeks in full-time training. Colin could not have known how hard it would be to win a regular place in the Premier League side. For everything was now clicking into place. Apart from a somewhat unhappy hiccough . . .

Clydebank 1 Hearts 0
28 September 1985

Of all clubs, Clydebank! I mean, what do you say to that? It's ridiculous. Of course, they're nice people and all that and they try very hard but by comparison with the Heart of Midlothian they are no more than a village side. I suppose that to be beaten by Clydebank, whether home or away or on the other side of the moon, the theory about football being a funny game is proved beyond all possible doubt.

At this point, perhaps, I should remember what I said—the car park job—when Forfar beat Hearts in the Cup. But it still shouldn't happen. It is STILL ridiculous.

Very well, even the Clydebank folk said Hearts were unlucky. And because they *are* nice people, they cannot be accused of having patronised us. Hearts did monopolise the game, as the home officials admitted with admirable frankness. A lot of good that did, didn't it? The attendance was 3,461.

I have no choice in this book but to mention these long gone times in the context of what we now know. I cannot apologise for that. It still brings an unbelieving shake of the head. A miserable 3,461! A far cry from the all-ticket situation that arose later on, wouldn't you say?

But the game itself is worthy of recall. And so is the overture to it.

Robertson and Clark play pig-in-the-middle
with a Clydebank defender

The manager, Alex MacDonald, had declared some time earlier in the season that he would play himself only in emergencies. He was looking on the game at Kilbowie Park, Clydebank, as a potential emergency. Kenny Black was under treatment and so were George Cowie and Roddy MacDonald. Craig Levein hadn't trained all week. Alex was quoted: "We just don't seem able to shake off injuries."

In the event the manager didn't play. He might have been

Black challenges the Clydebank defence

wishing he could have played as he sat in the dug-out wondering if Hearts were ever going to do anything at all outside shouting distance of Gorgie Road. The frustration must have been approaching the intolerable. It was what you might call a see-saw game. Hearts had plenty of chances and missed the lot. They were unquestionably in command so far as pressure and sheer aggression were concerned, but the Scottish League never did award two points for anything except goals. All the same, Hearts, while scoring no goals as the game wore on, were confidently expecting at least one point.

Even wee Alex, down in the dug-out, might have allowed himself a moment of relaxation as he looked at his watch and saw that there were only a couple of minutes to go. And that, with horrible inevitability, was when David Lloyd moved on to a cross from Marty Hughes and made Henry Smith wonder why he had ever taken up the profession of goalkeeping in the first place.

It gave Hearts no time at all to save the game, yet before Lloyd scored that winning goal—four minutes before, to be more precise—there ought to have been a penalty for Hearts when Jim Fallon's tackle on Sandy Clark was inside the box and outside the laws. John Colquhoun was in excellent form, without having anything to show for it. And there were even Hearts fans in the crowd who felt obliged to applaud the Clydebank goalkeeper, Jim Gallacher, for a spectacular save from a Sandy Clark header.

But only the Lloyd goal was marked in the referee's book. Nothing else, so far as the Premier League table was concerned, counted for anything.

Before we move on, however, we should listen to a few remarks from Sandy Jardine: "It's simply a matter of staying cool at a time when the little breaks are going against us. We're hoping that our luck will turn soon and that we can start picking up the points our performances are worth. The encouraging sign," Sandy added, "is that the players are putting in a tremendous amount of effort. In the end, they must be rewarded for their determination."

Think about that. Doesn't it make so much sense? And while

you're thinking, look also at the team that played against Clydebank. Wouldn't you say it was taking shape?

Clydebank: Gallacher; Dickson, Lloyd (sub 60 mins), Given, Fallon, Treanor, Maher, Ronald, Shanks, Larnach, Conroy, McCabe, Hughes (sub 15 mins).

Hearts: Smith: Kidd, Whittaker, S. Jardine, Berry, Levein, Colquhoun, Watson, Clark, Robertson, Black, MacDonald (sub 75 mins).

Referee: T. Muirhead, Stenhousemuir.

John Robertson's run is halted by Given.

Now we'll examine the Premier League table. Hearts remain with a pathetic five points after eight games. They have won two, drawn one and lost five. They have scored nine goals and they have conceded seventeen. They have played some good football, quite a lot of ordinary football, quite a lot of inferior football. They are probably worthy of a higher position in the table, but that could easily be arguable.

They have usually been determined without being very skilled, and their defence has been—with some glaring exceptions—better than either the midfield or the strikers. We have seen signs of improvement but too often these signs have been wiped out. The rest of the season does not look too good.

Naturally, the hard core of the fans will always be there, thank goodness. Thank somebody, anyway.

The next Premier League game for Hearts will be against Dundee at Tynecastle. The crowd is 8,500. They can now boast that they were in at the start of something good. There will be plenty who boast who weren't there, but what does that matter? The boys in maroon are poised to make Scottish football history.

It is surely the kind of history that will never be repeated. Just as well, one suspects, that the end of the trail cannot at this time be foreseen. Better to savour the joys as that history is made.

Hearts 1 Dundee 1
5 October 1985

It isn't much of a score-line, admittedly. But you know what they say about small beginnings.

The build-up to the game wasn't very promising, or so it seemed at the time. Roddy MacDonald and George Cowie were both definitely out and there was the sinister hoodoo of the Dundee club itself. In two Premier League seasons Hearts had beaten them only once. However, this is perhaps not the best time to discuss Dundee and the problems they have caused to Hearts. I would add that there may be a case for blowing up the Tay Bridge, but I fancy that I would then be accused of bad sportsmanship.

No, let's look at the game. Hearts played positively and nobody was more positive than Gary Mackay. He had been out of form and Alex MacDonald had relegated him to the reserves in

Colquhoun breaks clear at Dens, Jardine follows on.

the hope that he would recover his confidence. A foot injury had added to Gary's troubles. To his credit, he came back in this game to justify a selection that had appeared quite controversial.

John Robertson didn't find his scoring touch but still managed to keep the Dundee defence very concerned. So did Sandy Clark. John Colquhoun, if not as sharp as he could have been, was consistently menacing.

Dundee still scored first, though. Sandy Jardine, believe it or not, seemed vulnerable to untypical nervousness and made the error that left McWilliams quite unmarked. The lad didn't miss either. Sandy made up for it later on. He is the essential pro, above all. But it wasn't quite his day.

Dundee might have scored several afterwards but they didn't, and there was the clear impression left that the luck of the Hearts might be turning at long, long last. That impression was underlined when, after Ian Jardine equalised from a Colquhoun cross, Craig Levein up-ended McWilliams with no ceremony at

89

all, right there in the penalty box. I thought it was a penalty. I'm sure Alex MacDonald thought it was a penalty. Just about everybody thought it was a penalty. "Carry on regardless," ruled the referee, a man of perception, vision, compassion, common sense and indeed innumerable virtues. If Dundee fans do not agree with that, tough!

"Well," said Alex MacDonald, "at least we stopped losing silly goals late in the game. When you remember how we have been faring against Dundee for the last few years, this point is a bonus really."

The Dundee manager, Archie Knox, was in philosophical mood after he had verbally blasted his players for about half-an-hour. "A point at Tynecastle isn't so bad," he said.

Anybody who believes that Archie Knox can ever be happy with one point anywhere, and I do not except Real Madrid, Barcelona and Liverpool, must also believe that goalposts are made of sugar.

As any goalie will tell you, they're not.

Hearts:	Smith: Kidd, Whittaker, S. Jardine, Berry, Levein, Colquhoun, Black (sub 73 mins), I. Jardine, Clark, Mackay, Robertson.
Dundee:	Geddes: Shannon, Glennie, McCormack, Smith, Duffy, Rafferty, Hendry, Harvey, Connor, McWilliams.
Referee:	A. Ferguson, Giffnock.

Celtic 0 Hearts 1
12 October 1985

Before this game Celtic had been unbeaten, and only clairvoyants and Hearts fans (not all of them, either) would have gambled on their losing that record. But Hearts battled nobly . . . "battled" was the verb perhaps most frequently used about Hearts as the season progressed, not only at Tynecastle but by managers of teams wishing they could bottle some of that battle.

Of course, Celtic did not go down lightly. They never do, do they? But their finishing owed little to either luck or accuracy, with Mo Johnston particularly culpable. Mo was scarcely helped by the burgeoning talent of Craig Levein, whose speed and vision was already marking him out as a potential internationalist.

Thus, while Celtic attacked more or less non-stop for long spells, it was all huffing and puffing and not much else. Towards the end Celtic grew increasingly frantic and Hearts grew increasingly confident, even if the rearguard action was grim at times. In the game against Celtic at Tynecastle the previous March, referee Brian McGinlay had played five minutes extra in order to counter what were surely "stalling" home tactics. Brian McClair had then scored a winner. The second-half of this match lasted for 51 minutes, not really because Hearts were again trying it on, but because John Robertson, who had scored the 33rd-minute winner, was later hurt and medical attention took some time. That was an anxious episode for Hearts and I don't suppose wee John was too pleased either—when he woke up.

He was carried off unconscious, with a collar round his neck, after a collision with Roy Aitken. It was feared at first that his neck might be broken but in hospital the injury was diagnosed as a pinched nerve in the throat. Sandy Jardine said afterwards, with feeling: "We got the fright of our lives when they took John away, but I stress that it was all accidental."

It is worth recalling now that, in the *Evening News* on the Monday, Ian McNiven wrote: "I have always said Hearts were capable of beating anybody in the Premier League. They have the right qualities to keep battling when the odds are against them. Only constant changes forced by injuries and suspensions have prevented them picking up more points in the first quarter of the programme."

Celtic: Bonner: McGrain, Aitken, McCugan, Burns, Grant, McStay, MacLeod, Provan, Johnston, McClair.

Hearts: Smith: Kidd, S. Jardine, Levein, Whittaker, I. Jardine, Berry, Mackay, Colquhoun, Black (sub 61 mins), Clark, Robertson, Watson (sub 74 mins).

Referee: Jim Duncan, Gorebridge.

Hearts 3 St Mirren 0
19 October 1985

Two young Hearts stars had been in the news. John Robertson, inevitably, after that injury at Parkhead. But he was still fit to play against St Mirren. And Craig Levein, subject of a reported £250,000 offer from Aston Villa. Chairman Wallace Mercer, however, scorned both the report and the amount: "It's a joke." And so Hearts were able to field the side that had beaten Celtic. Things were certainly on the mend, in more ways than one.

Anyway, this victory was composed by virtue of the most attractive football Hearts had played all season up to that time. Ian Jardine, Gary Mackay and John Colquhoun made enterprising contributions and the team as a whole moved sweetly in midfield, attacked with vigour and menace, and defended without making too many compromises. Craig Levein, in fact, was cautioned early on, after he had challenged Frank McGarvey with rather too much exuberance. After the match manager Alex MacDonald named Henry Smith as his No. 1 Hearts player, almost certainly because of the confidence filtering from the unflappable Henry right through the defence.

But Alex couldn't have been too displeased with the goals, either. Two typical pieces of opportunism from John Robertson and an equally typical spectacular goal from Gary Mackay, who created space for himself before delivering a vicious right-foot shot from 20 yards out.

Hearts:	Smith: Kidd, S. Jardine, Levein, Whittaker, I. Jardine, Berry, Mackay, Colquhoun, Clark, Robertson.
St Mirren:	Money: Cooper, Godfrey, Clarke, Hamilton, Fitzpatrick, Rooney, Mackie (sub 72 mins), McDowall, Speirs, Abercromby (sub 72 mins), Gallacher, McGarvey.
Referee:	J. Renton, Cowdenbeath.

Hearts now had no Premier League fixture for ten days as, on October 27, their scheduled opponents, Aberdeen, were too busy slaughtering Hibs in the League Cup Final at Hampden. This slight postponement didn't suit Hearts, who were obviously hoping to maintain momentum, but it might have been worse.

Aberdeen actually asked the Scottish League to put back the league fixture even further, because of what they saw as pressures on them . . . 18 games in 11 weeks. That was turned down. Presumably the League took the view that a club of Aberdeen's stature should have a first-team pool big enough for such contingencies.

Hearts 1 Aberdeen 0
30 October 1985

It had been seven years since Hearts last beat Aberdeen in a league game at Tynecastle. A long wait, indeed, but this success was no less deserved for that.

Craig Levein showed how well he fitted his under-21 international cap with a brilliant performance, itself "capped" by the goal that was destined to win the match. It came in the 15th minute, after a spell in which Hearts had always looked more fluid. Levein beat Jim Leighton in the air and headed in a Colquhoun corner-kick. It is not usual for Scotland's first-choice goalkeeper to make mistakes in the air . . . but then, neither is it

Celebration time against Aberdeen in a league match

Henry saves–again!

usual for Willie Miller to be unreliable. Aberdeen's captain was clearly distressed by the way Colquhoun, Robertson and Mackay ran at his defence, and Alex McLeish wasn't very happy about it either.

The crowd was 12,446 on a rainy Wednesday night, not bad in the circumstances, if not of a size that would have been acceptable a couple of months or so later. More importantly, they went home highly delighted. It had been a cliffhanger, with the Dons predictably annoyed by the impending loss of their record, attacking with every resource in the final quarter-hour. Their efforts didn't die out until the bitter end—which was almost exactly when Henry Smith brought off a save, from Neil Simpson, that had the fans making partisan comparisons with Leighton.

Alex Ferguson, though, was generous in his praise of Hearts. "When Hearts are playing like that," he said, "and with Hibs and

St Mirren climbing up the League, you just can't assume any point is won."

Hearts:	Smith: Kidd, Whittaker, S. Jardine, Berry, Levein, Colquhoun, I. Jardine, Black (sub 75 mins), Clark, Robertson, Mackay.
Aberdeen:	Leighton: McKimmie, Angus, Bett (sub 60 mins), Gray, McLeish, Miller, Weir, Simpson, McDougall, Wright (sub 66 mins), Cooper, Hewitt.
Referee:	L. Thow, Ayr.

Henry's high against Dundee United

Dundee United 1 Hearts 1
2 November 1985

Football writers were now beginning to talk of the "new Hearts". Possibly this was premature and one doubts if it was even accurate. Crucially, the Hearts were now able to field a more settled side. Certainly they ought to have won at Tannadice and the fact that they failed to do so was entirely due to their forgetting a basic rule. That is, never to relax until the referee makes it official.

United, frankly, looked ragged, which is not their style at all, whether at Tannadice or anywhere else. But it is fair to ask why. It is also fair to suggest that Hearts made them look ragged.

Gary Mackay, Ian Jardine and Neil Berry were outstanding in midfield, enabling Hearts to produce creative, attractive football. Jardine, that magnificent striker of a ball, got the goal which for so long seemed to be the winner. After 67 minutes, Colquhoun, Mackay and Berry combined in a move that saw Ian racing on to the ball just outside the box. It is questionable whether Thomson, in the United goal, even saw the shot.

But there was nothing wrong with the United equaliser, and never mind even if it *was* scored in injury-time. Eamonn Bannon, whose departure from Tynecastle a few years ago occasioned much distress among the Hearts faithful, directed a pass from nearly 40 yards right into the path of the eagerly sprinting Paul Sturrock. Richard Gough kept pace, which couldn't have been easy, and headed in Sturrock's cross.

"Now that is the best Hearts' side for a long time," said Jim McLean after the game. "They're taking points from the top teams, and that opens up the League. They bring plenty of fans with them, too, which means more cash for football."

The Tannadice attendance was 10,142. Probably half were shouting for Hearts. Yes indeed, Hearts were being noticed.

Dundee United: Thomson: Malpas, Holt, Gough, Hegarty, Narey, Bannon, Milne, Dodds, Sturrock, Redford, Beedie (sub 45 mins).

Hearts: Smith: Kidd, Whittaker, S. Jardine, Berry, Levein, Colquhoun, I. Jardine, Clark, Mackay, Robertson, Black (sub 40 mins).

Referee: R. Valentine, Dundee.

Maybe it's time for another look at the Premier League table, the next match being against Hibs at Easter Road. Hearts have 13 points from 13 games played. Hibs have 13 points from 12 games. Nobody is predicting anything yet. Not with Aberdeen five points ahead and threatening to open up a formidable gap.

Hibs 0 Hearts 0
9 November 1985

The trouble with almost any local derby is the fear of losing—a fear usually distributed equally among both sides. So much is at stake in terms of local prestige—which can sometimes count for more than points.

That is not an attitude calculated to produce thoughtful football. The overriding aim is to thump the ball as far away from one's own goal as possible—and as quickly as possible. The atmosphere also tends to mean extra work for the referee. This is exactly how things worked out at Easter Road.

John Blackley commented afterwards: "A good game between two in-form teams. Both sides showed a lot of pride and no quarter was asked or given."

Well, I'm not sure about the first part of John's summing-up, but he was right about no quarter being asked. It certainly wasn't. Six players were booked: Whittaker, Levein and Ian Jardine of Hearts, and Rae, Brazil and Kane of Hibs.

"Another blood and thunder derby, with both sides happy to settle for a point." That was one press verdict, and fair enough too. But the fans still left, talking about the easiest chance of the match. It fell to Sandy Clark 15 minutes from the end.

Robertson and Mackay set up the opportunity for big Sandy, who had been the Tynecastle side's busiest attacker. But he appeared to stumble on the wet surface and, from the end of the six-yard box, thumped the ball into the side net. Alan Rough, who had an international-class game, could hardly believe his luck.

Hibs:	Rough: Sneddon, Munro, Rae, Fulton, Hunter, Kane, Chisholm, Cowan, Durie, McBride, Brazil (sub 49 mins).
Hearts:	Smith: Kidd, Whittaker, S. Jardine, Levein, Berry, Colquhoun, Black (sub 66 mins), I. Jardine, Clark, Mackay, Robertson.
Referee:	G. Smith, Edinburgh.

Another statistic, and a happy one. Sandy Jardine, assistant-manager of Hearts and now playing some of the most effective football of his career as sweeper, is about to mark up his 1,000th senior appearance. By what seems like a sort of divine conspiracy, Sandy's 1,000th game will be against . . . Rangers! Sandy has been in the game for more than 18 years and shows every sign of continuing for some time yet.

Hearts 3 Rangers 0
16 November 1985

Sandy Jardine was presented with some Edinburgh crystal to celebrate that 1,000th game and a press box wit asked if there was any chance of his transfer back to Rangers. Indeed a joke, but it needn't have been.

Rangers sorely needed a defender of real class on the evidence of this display. Hearts could not claim to have turned in a brilliant performance, but brilliance was not required. And we are talking about a Rangers team that had just soundly beaten Celtic!

But this was no contest. There wasn't much entertaining football, and what there was came from Hearts, who seemed unable to understand why Rangers were so easy to beat. There was no score at half-time, but that was principally due to the usually sharp John Robertson passing up a couple of easy chances. Rangers had been virtually besieged and could do nothing about it.

Sandy Clark, however, was clearly fed up with the situation He had no intention of allowing his former team-mates to escape, and his industry was admirable. It was appropriately rewarded when he lobbed in a 57th minute goal and, about 20 minutes later, he strolled over to a John Colquhoun centre and scored with an almost contemptuous casualness. Robertson made it three with a header on the turn that needed courage as well as timing, but few were in any doubt about the outstanding Hearts man. That honour had to go to Walter Kidd, with Neil Berry not far behind.

I appreciated the honesty of Jock Wallace's summing-up. "If you don't tackle or fight, then you don't win. We were completely outplayed."

Berry uses his head against Rangers

Hearts: Smith: Kidd, S. Jardine, Levein, Whittaker, I. Jardine, Mackay, Berry, Colquhoun, Clark, Robertson.

Rangers: Walker: Dawson, MacKinnon, McPherson, Munro, Russell, Bell, Burns (sub 81 mins), Durrant, McCoist, Williamson, McMinn (sub 63 mins), Cooper.

Referee: T. Muirhead, Stenhousemuir.

Hearts 3 Motherwell 0
23 November 1985

On this Saturday morning Hearts had been unbeaten in seven consecutive matches and the average Tynecastle attendance was now 14,500. Alex MacDonald was admitting, very cautiously, that his aim was a high place in the League, a place in Europe, and a good run in the Cup . . .

By a quarter-to-five that afternoon, Hearts were fourth top of the League, with 18 points from 16 games, three behind Aberdeen.

99

Motherwell provided scant opposition here, and after losing their striker, Raymond Blair, four minutes before half-time, provided just about no opposition at all. Raymond, though, had only himself to blame. He has a rather low boiling-point and the referee became highly upset after his second bad foul. That was a red-card job and the wonder was that Hearts managed to score only three in the end. I know there's no point in crying about it now, but another half-dozen, eminently feasible, would have done no harm at all to the final tally.

But despite their domination—with everybody bar Henry Smith able and willing to attack—not enough chances were made, much less taken. Sandy Clark had got the first goal after half-an-hour, then knocked in another after 56 minutes. That came from a Colquhoun cross. If I had a month or so to spare, I'd analyse the Hearts goals and work out how many resulted from a Colquhoun pass. I'm convinced there would be an extremely high percentage. The third goal fell to Ian Jardine, shooting with fine force and precision.

Hearts:	Smith: Kidd, S. Jardine, Levein, Black, I. Jardine, Mackay, Berry, Colquhoun, Clark, Robertson.
Motherwell:	Gardiner: Wishart, Forbes, McCart, Murray, Kennedy (sub 61 mins), Dornan, Macleod, Wright, Gahagan, Harrow, Reilly (sub 68 mins), Blair.
Referee:	H. Williamson, Renfrew.

A sense of excitement was now obvious among the Tynecastle fans. Not at Tynecastle itself, you understand. Alex MacDonald and Sandy Jardine stayed cool, placid almost. "One game at a time" seemed to be the MacDonald theme-song. But not even the managerial team could have failed to notice that a victory over Clydebank would place Hearts second top.

For this was the only Premier League game on the card, owing to the World Cup play-off in Australia.

Hearts 4 Clydebank 1
30 November 1985

Tynecastle was frost-bound and treacherous—the game must

have come close to postponement—but Hearts didn't have any problems as they achieved their first-ever Premier League win over Clydebank. It was a nasty day for the spectators, by the way, but the attendance was 10,267—more than the total for the seven-match First Division programme played that day.

Clydebank were second bottom of the League, Hearts almost at the top. That gap was emphasised almost from the start. Everything went smoothly for Hearts, frost or no frost, with Sandy Jardine conducting proceedings as if he were on a rostrum with a baton.

Clark gets his shot in despite Auld's tackle

When Neil Berry scored after five minutes—his first goal for Hearts, incidentally—the only question was, how many? In ideal conditions, Hearts might, in fact, have piled up an embarrassing total. As it was, Clydebank knew they were fortunate to go down by a score that was at least comparatively respectable.

One headline said, on the Sunday: "Yes, Hearts do look like champions!" One cannot know who wrote that headline, but it is reasonable to presume that he was brought up in the East of Scotland, maybe even around Tranent or Gorebridge. Maybe, let's face it, in the vicinity of Gorgie Road itself.

In any event, it was a beautiful thought.

It was given additional inspiration by the rest of the goals. Colquhoun crossed—yes, the wee man, again—in the 41st minute, and Sandy Clark made something of a fool of the defence as he turned and scored easily. Sandy was showing a subtlety here which had not always been obvious in his play. It was no less appreciated for that. Clark and Mackay did the work for Robertson to score a third—but bear in mind, he *did* score. Countless chances are lost by strikers, whatever the effort that preceded the chance. Given fouled Robertson, quite blatantly, in the box, after 77 minutes, and up went Kenny Black to rattle in the penalty. Four minutes from the end, Hughes got one for Clydebank but did not succeed in dampening the spirits of the home support. And the rain was teeming down now.

It was quite promising all the same to note, courtesy of the manager, that the Hearts players had been quite upset by that goal.

Hearts:	Smith: Kidd, Black, S. Jardine, Berry, Levein, Colquhoun, I. Jardine, Clark, Mackay, Robertson.
Clydebank:	Gallacher: Treanor, Given, Maher, Auld, McGhie, Ronald, Hughes (sub 73 mins), Shanks, Larnach, Conroy (sub 59 mins), Bain, McCabe.
Referee:	D. Yeats, Perth.

The next game was against Dundee at Dens Park, a dangerous situation, even then. We couldn't see into the future. We were sick and tired of the very name of Dundee, an attitude understandable if one remembers that, in nine championship games between the two clubs, Dundee had lost only one. Strangely, we didn't object too strongly—even if we didn't like it—to being messed about by Dundee United, the vastly superior team in that city. It was annoying to be caused so much inconvenience by the Dens Park lot.

It was to continue, even so, and for far, far too long. It was not yet the ambition of all right-thinking Hearts supporters to consign Dundee to a lower division, but that very ambition was certainly being formed. Like a bluebottle at a window pane on a summer's day, Dundee were a very great pain in the backside.

So we were now about to go to Dens Park, and the incentive for victory was very obvious. Aberdeen had no Premier League game, so Hearts were on the verge of the league leadership.

Dundee 1 Hearts 1
7 December 1985

So Dundee frustrated Hearts yet again. Earlier in this book, I suggested that there might be a case for getting rid of the Tay Bridge. It was now about time to consider getting rid of Dundee altogether. What a shame, we thought, that Dens was so close to Tannadice. How to atomise one, without the other!

Only by a tiny goal difference did Hearts fail to take over the top of the Premier League. It was all very well for Archie Knox

Walter Kidd gets his cross in against Dundee

to praise the huge Hearts support at Dens. It didn't do Hearts nearly enough good, considering that there couldn't have been more than a few dozen Dundee fans at the match. All the cash went into the home coffers but that, of course, is the cross which must be borne by well-supported clubs.

It is annoying that clubs like Dundee, in a city which clearly prefers to watch snooker, darts and bowls, should benefit so greatly. But not much can be done about that, I suppose. It has to be better than giving them half of the home gates.

Whatever, Dundee had the impertinence to go one up within only seven minutes. At the same time, it should be conceded that Henry Smith didn't do too well when trying to punch clear a free-kick from Jim Smith. John Brown was given too much time as he collected the clearance and, from 18 yards, hit the ball back at Henry—and past him.

That was quite bad enough. But then, quite near to half-time, Kenny Black missed a penalty. Kenny, whose usual ploy is to take both goalkeeper and net into the next county, tried to place the ball with delicacy. Geddes saw it coming, and said, "Thank you very much".

Ian Jardine then did the business, as they say. He had never played in a losing Hearts side, and it was almost a matter of honour to him that he should preserve that record.

There were only ten minutes left and the game seemed in grave jeopardy. This, despite the undeniable superiority of Hearts.

In midfield, Dundee were not at the races. Jim Duffy, that excellent defender, has seldom played better, otherwise there would have been no need for Ian Jardine's anxiety. However, Ian stepped in at a free-kick, saw it blocked, and was grateful for a second chance. That one, he didn't miss.

Dundee:	Geddes: Shannon, Glennie, Rafferty, Smith, Duffy, Stephen, Brown, Hendry (sub 60 mins), Harvey, Connor, Jack, Kidd (sub 79 mins).
Hearts:	Smith: Kidd, Black, S. Jardine, Whittaker (sub 39 mins), Berry, Levein, Colquhoun, I. Jardine, Clark, Mackay, Watson (sub 58 mins), Robertson.
Referee:	J. Duncan, Gorebridge.

After all this Messrs MacDonald and Jardine refused to say a word to the newspapers about the possibility of a championship win. They were second from the top, fair enough, and second by only goals not points, but, to quote Sandy Jardine: "If we're in the same position, with eight games to go, then we'd be in with a definite chance. What we won't do, is to put pressure on the younger players. It's one Saturday after the other, as far as we're concerned."

Coming up to Christmas, there were, of course, a lot more than eight games to go. . . .

Hearts 1 Celtic 1
14 December 1985

Hearts have now won more points at home than any other Premier League side. They have a good chance of going to the top of the League. They don't blow it, if that phrase can be translated as making too many mistakes. They still don't quite make it . . .

There were no fewer than 20,000 fans inside the ground at the kick-off, and there were quite a lot more trying to get in, queueing, frustrated and angry. This has often been a source of complaints from visiting Celtic and Rangers fans but, as has been often explained, no stadium in Scotland can cope with a surge of thousands of customers within the space of ten minutes or so. By the same token, is a commercial enterprise entitled to ask the public to leave the pub long before the game starts? It's a good question. It is certainly not confined to Tynecastle.

Be that as it may, Hearts stretched their unbeaten run to eleven, and might well have done so with a win rather than with a draw. The referee, Glasgow's Mr Syme made several decisions which were incomprehensible to the home punters, and which left Hearts with a sense of irritation, if not of persecution. We all know how easy, how tempting it is, to criticise referees, but this was definitely not one of Mr Syme's better days. And he is surely one of Scotland's best . . .

The game itself would not have aroused much enthusiasm

among connoisseurs. Elegant football was simply not on, and the duel between Roy Aitken and Sandy Clark was a very long way from being a football version of chess. Luckily, the pair understood each other, and neither was the type to bleat.

Sandy Jardine, sweeping with his customary coolness, stepped in to clear up an untypical blunder by Neil Berry, and that helped to settle Hearts. Aitken gave away a corner, harrassed by Mackay. Black took a short one, Colquhoun collected calmly, and crossed nicely to John Robertson. Thus, within ten minutes Hearts were one up.

There wasn't much to talk about, apart from the referee, before Mark McGhee scored from a pass by Mo Johnston, in the 66th minute.

Hearts: Smith: Kidd, Levein, S. Jardine, Black, I. Jardine, Mackay, Berry, Colquhoun, Robertson, Watson (sub 75 mins), Clark.
Celtic: Bonner: Grant, Aitken, McCugan, Burns, McClair, McStay, MacLeod, Johnston, McGhee, Archdeacon.
Referee: D. Syme, Glasgow.

Hearts were now unbeaten since the beginning of October, and had been watched by an average of 15,000 in these 11 games. Sandy Jardine had the right words: "Supporters are bringing their mates to Tynecastle, and youngsters are bringing parents—not the other way round all the time. There's a buzz about Edinburgh. We're not only getting results, we're playing good football."

Sandy was speaking about the unbeaten run, in general terms, of course. He was not, by any standards, pointing to the Celtic game as an example of good football. Few folk, after all, were better qualified to discuss the class stuff.

St Mirren 0 Hearts 1
21 December 1985

So there it is. For the first time since 1973, the Heart of Midlothian Football Club is at the top of the Premier League.

It is not unexpected. It is richly merited.

They now have 24 points from 20 matches, one more than

Aberdeen. True, Aberdeen have a game in hand at this point, but as any fan will agree, it's better to have the points in the bag. Not even Aberdeen fans would argue with that . . .

Hearts beat St Mirren at Paisley only by virtue of a penalty-kick. But it wasn't the first big game to be settled by a penalty and it won't be the last.

Ironically, St Mirren had a fair claim to a penalty that would have—or could have—been an equaliser. Their manager Alex Miller, seemed greatly disturbed, when the referee decided that there was nothing wrong with Kenny Black's tackle on Neil Cooper. That was very close to the end. The ref was booed off the field, and only the most partisan Hearts fan could have disagreed with this reaction.

But it's the old swings-and-roundabouts game, isn't it? Win a few, lose a few! In the 25th minute, Hearts had won one . . . when Billy Abercromby took the view that Gary Mackay had no right to a clear shot at goal. A penalty, and who scored? Who else but Kenny Black.

St Mirren showed a lot of fight over the piece but never looked really capable of giving Hearts a problem . . . the disputed penalty excepted. That point was underlined by the fact that Henry Smith had one of his easiest afternoons for quite some time.

St Mirren:	Money: Wilson, Abercromby, Godfrey, Cooper, Fitzpatrick, Winnie, Rooney, McGarvey, Gallacher, Speirs.
Hearts:	Smith: Kidd, Black, S. Jardine, Levein, Berry, I. Jardine, Mackay, Colquhoun, Robertson, Clark.
Referee:	A. Huett, Airdrie.

I liked the comment on the Monday morning from Hugh Keevins in the *Scotsman.* He wrote: "Hearts are at present the best team in the country. The results speak for themselves, and the Premier Division table offers visual proof for the hard of hearing."

Few football clubs take account of the festive season. This was Christmas week. But apart from Christmas Day itself, there was no extra day off for the boys in maroon at the top of the League. "The time to celebrate Christmas, if we have the chance," said Sandy Jardine, "is in the early summer."

Rangers 0 Hearts 2

28 December 1985

No change in the Hearts line up . . . and that's not just mere team news. After the disappointing start to the season, when Alex MacDonald couldn't pick the same side twice, a settled team was an enormous bonus.

Rangers became the latest team to appreciate as much, to their cost.

It really wasn't too difficult for Hearts. They were superbly organised, whereas Rangers had nobody who mattered in midfield.

Hearts had their usual midfield men, tackling as tenaciously as ever, backing each other up, creating chances with superb speed of thought and economy of moves. Generally, indeed, this Hearts team now knew how good it was, and a confrontation with Rangers at Ibrox mattered no more than one with Clydebank at Tynecastle.

This was not an under-estimation of Rangers. It was a realistic view of comparative worth.

From a more individualistic outlook, it was John Colquhoun's day—although Neil Berry, too, couldn't have missed a square inch of Ibrox, as he helped to ensure that any Ibrox attacking ambitions were nipped off at source. And Ian Jardine's long passing was exemplary.

Colquhoun scored both goals, each the reward of being in the right spot at the right time—and you don't arrive at such a situation by accident. He helped Sandy Clark to cause havoc in the Ibrox defence, and John Robertson was always following up to cause a bit more.

Thanks to Colquhoun, Hearts were two ahead within 25 minutes and while never forgetting that Rangers were normally liable to fight back hard, the possibility of any reverse was not taken seriously. In the run of 12 matches undefeated, after all, Hearts had conceded only five goals. The run has now stretched to 13. So much for superstition!

Rangers: Walker: Dawson, Munro, McPherson, Paterson, Durrant, McCoist, Russell, Nisbet, D. Ferguson, Cooper.
Hearts: Smith: Kidd, Black, S. Jardine, Berry, Levein, Colquhoun, I. Jardine, Clark, Mackay, Robertson.
Referee: W. P. Knowles, Inverurie.

Hearts 3 Hibs 1
1 January 1986

It is always highly acceptable to beat Hibs, if I may be permitted to speak as someone with an affection for Hearts, but oh, what extra fun it is to beat them on New Year's Day. It adds a certain piquancy to the festive season, doesn't it?

The Tynecastle attendance was 27,500, and the vast majority of that crowd stayed at the end to give Hearts what is called in political circles a standing ovation.

Alex MacDonald could now look back and say that as

Sandy Clark gets in a shot against Aberdeen

109

manager he had never lost a match against Hibs, and he certainly never seemed likely to lose this one.

Levein, Ian Jardine, Berry and Mackay shoved the game into their pockets, so to speak, and kept it there. And Walter Kidd was absolutely inspiring in his role as captain.

Hibs tried hard. Against Hearts they always try hard. Otherwise, they'd probably be lynched—and it would be a similar situation, if any Hearts player were ever noted to be giving less than 100 per cent.

But there's a big difference between effort and achievement.

Overall, Hibs were outplayed, although the match—unlike the previous derby at Easter Road—did provide a fine quota of entertaining football.

Ian Jardine scored first in the 25th minute, gratefully accepting a free-kick from Gary Mackay, placed fastidiously into his path.

Rough, in the Hibs goal, proceeded to make a clown of his critics—not for the first time—as Hearts became more and more aggressive, but he didn't have much chance when John Robertson swept in a Kenny Black pass. Time 71 minutes.

Three more minutes, two more goals . . . a looping header from Harris, and a close-range hook from Sandy Clark after a Colquhoun-Robertson move.

After the game, in the press room, I was pleased with the opportunity to wish John Blackley a Happy New Year. He took it well.

Hearts: Smith: Kidd, Black, S. Jardine, Berry, Levein, Colquhoun, I. Jardine, Clark, Mackay, Robertson.

Hibs: Rough: Sneddon, Brazil, Rae, Fulton, Hunter, Kane, Chisholm, Cowan, Harris, Tortalano, May (sub 61 mins).

Referee: R. Valentine, Dundee.

Motherwell 1 Hearts 3
4 January 1986

This was again the kind of weather guaranteed to test any team with ambition—of which Hearts by now, had plenty. The Fir

Park pitch was snow-bound, and while the falling snow could hardly be classed as a blizzard, it was obviously more of a hindrance than a help. Motherwell had their backs to the snow in the first-half, which perhaps explained why they managed to claim enough of the play to score. That was when Reilly collected a throw-in and hit a fine shot past Smith from 18 yards.

In ideal conditions and with reasonable visibility, Henry might still have saved that one, but there's no point in making excuses. They're not necessary anyway. Hearts went on in the second-half to win quite comfortably and certainly on merit. Ten minutes after the interval, Ian Jardine punished a careless pass-back to equalise and, almost immediately, Berry made an impeccable job of completing a pleasant move from Clark and Robertson. Robertson got the third five minutes from the end—to ensure a 15th game without defeat.

"People had better start taking Hearts seriously," said Jim McLean that weekend. "They have marvellous travelling support and outnumber most fans."

If it should be thought that Jim was emphasising the supporting element too heavily—and forgetting the players— I have to say that this was not the first time the Dundee United manager had praised Hearts. Undoubtedly a man with a feeling for football . . .

Motherwell:	Gardiner: Wishart, Boyd, McCart, MacLeod, Dornan, Blair (sub 67 mins), Doyle, Wright, McStay, Reilly, Mulvanney.
Hearts:	Smith: Kidd, S. Jardine, Levein, Black, I. Jardine, Berry, Mackay, Colquhoun, McAdam (sub 81 mins), Clark, Robertson.
Referee:	K. O'Donnell, Airdrie.

The draw for the third round of the Scottish Cup was now known. Only two Premier League clubs were paired: Hearts and Rangers at Tynecastle. Some Hearts, maybe many Hearts fans, might have been wishing for a less demanding start on the way to Hampden. Oh, they of little faith!

Hearts 1 Dundee United 1
11 January 1986

This Premier League point brought the Hearts unbeaten total to 16, and the draw kept Dundee United's title hopes alive.

But the statistic that caused as much talk as any other was the attendance—19,043, in appalling conditions. United's reputation for turning on entertaining football was presumably an important factor, but there remained the suspicion that Hearts would now attract a tolerable gate if opposed to eleven dustbins. The bandwagon wasn't just rolling, it was getting into overdrive.

It was good to see Gary Mackay emerge as the hero of Hearts—his form had been a shade spotty—and he deserved praise as much for his character as for his skill. Not many lads of his age could have recovered so dramatically after missing a penalty kick. Which was exactly what Gary did—it was an excellent save by Thomson—and at the worst possible time for Hearts. A minute before half-time! Gary proceeded, in the second-half, to contribute superbly in a spell that demonstrated the worth of the Tynecastle midfield. Then, just past the hour, he controlled smoothly a headed pass from Clark and with equal smoothness, took a certain revenge on Thomson. Nobody could argue with the quality of Bannon's equalising goal on the 70-minute mark—a quite spectacular volley. But as to whether United deserved a point in the end . . . that was another matter altogether.

Hearts:	Smith: Kidd, Whittaker, S. Jardine, Levein, Berry, Colquhoun, Black, Clark, Mackay, Robertson.
Dundee United:	Thomson: Malpas, Beaumont, Gough, Hegarty, Narey, Bannon, Gallacher, Redford, Coyne (sub 58 mins), Sturrock, Dodds.
Referee:	D. McVicar, Calrule.

Aberdeen 0 Hearts 1
18 January 1986

Well if anybody wasn't taking Hearts seriously now, he must have been a Hibbie (his own team having 18 points from 22 games).

A scramble for the ball in a league match against Aberdeen

However, what was definitely not taken seriously was the chance of history repeating itself—the last time Hearts had won at Pittodrie, they finished the season relegated!

And yet I admitted at the time, so I won't fudge the issue now, I was surprised by this victory. I did think Hearts would survive undefeated, but the extra point meant so much ... from the viewpoint of morale as well as mathematics. And Hearts came home with 33 points from 25 matches—four more than Dundee United who had played three fewer games. And five more than Celtic who had played two fewer.

By the way, Hearts did nothing at Pittodrie to let anybody suspect their morale was suspect. Far from it! Their self-assurance was widely commented on. But it doesn't do any harm to beat the reigning champions on their own ground, does it?

And their success was deserved well enough. Aberdeen hadn't lost at home for 13 months, something which troubled

Hearts not at all. Maybe the maroons did start with a touch of nerves, but very soon—once again—that midfield was taking over. Dons claimed a bigger share of the proceedings after the interval, and there wasn't a Hearts fan in the place who wouldn't have settled for a draw. Not Alex MacDonald, though.

John Robertson had been playing unusually deep, and when he was taken off in favour of big Colin McAdam—who was given a hard striking role—it became clear that Hearts were out to *win*. The substitution was made in the 81st minute. A couple of minutes later, Kidd moved powerfully forward and gave John Colquhoun a chance which the little man took with great confidence.

Aberdeen: Leighton: McKimmie, McLeish, W. Miller, McQueen, Mitchell (sub 68 mins), Stark, Simpson, Bett, Black, McDougall, J. Miller (sub 70 mins), Weir.

Hearts: Smith: Kidd, S. Jardine, Levein, Black, I. Jardine, Berry, Mackay, Colquhoun, Clark, Robertson, McAdam (sub 81 mins).

We take a break for the Cup, and the all-ticket tie with Rangers. Expectations are for an old-fashioned battle. But for Hearts fans, who are optimistic above all about the championship, this tie is like a sort of holiday away from the tension. A bonus, in a way. For the Rangers supporters, recognising that the title is a forlorn hope, it's much different. Defeat . . . and the rest of the season could be dead.

Hearts 3 Rangers 2
25 January 1986

The *Sunday Mail* headline said: "Classy maroons grab glory in capital cracker". There seemed to be no reason to debate that assessment.

Hearts showed more class than Rangers, they did indeed grab the glory, and it was undeniably a cracker of a game. And yet, while not easy, it was just about possible to feel a teeny-weeny pang of sympathy for Rangers. They didn't have much luck.

Hail victory!
Levein and McAdam signal triumph over Rangers

At the same time, perhaps we should remember that over more than a century of football Rangers have enjoyed more good fortune on the field than any other Scottish Club, with Celtic not far behind.

It was unlucky for Hearts, as it happened, when McCoist put Rangers in front, just before half-time. Rangers had made no other chances until that point. They were missing Paterson, injured after half-an-hour, but Hearts lost Clark in the same collision.

It was a tough, bruising game by any standards, but I still recall feeling fairly confident at the interval. Hearts were much more creative, and that had to pay off, sooner or later. Sooner, as it happened. McAdam equalised in the 49th minute—his first goal for Hearts—and a few minutes later, Mackay thumped in a corner from Colquhoun. Smith and Levein got into an embarrassing mix-up, which permitted Durrant to make it two each in the 69th minute, but the cheering had hardly died down when Ferguson was sent off for retaliation against Mackay. Hearts exploited the Ibrox handicap with renewed pressure— and there was no time for a Rangers recovery when Robertson sent Tynecastle wild with delight. John had had very few chances in the previous 85 minutes. Nobody cared about that now!

Hearts: Smith: Kidd, Black, S. Jardine, Levein, Berry, Colquhoun, I. Jardine, Clark, McAdam (sub 30 mins), Mackay, Robertson.

Rangers: Walker: Burns, Miller, Dawson, Paterson, Russell (sub 30 mins), Durrant, McCoist, D. Ferguson, Williamson, McPherson, Cooper.

Referee: T. Muirhead, Stenhousemuir.

Clydebank 1 Hearts 1
1 February 1986

After Hearts had maintained their Premier League record at Kilbowie—now 18 in succession without defeat—that gifted Clydebank play-maker Gerry McCabe gave it as his considered opinion that Hearts did not look like championship material.

Gerry more than most was entitled to an opinion. We wonder if he was revising it later on, though.

Levein puts Aberdeen under pressure

As usual Clydebank gave Hearts plenty of problems, and came very close to giving them a problem too many.

Craig Levein had been suspended, and he was always bound to be missed, but in this type of game, Roddy MacDonald was to be relied upon all the way. Roddy shouldn't see that as faint praise. I cordially share Alex MacDonald's high regard for him.

It was the kind of struggle usually described as dour. Ironically, it was McCabe himself who missed an open goal in the 60th minute. Ten minutes earlier he had made one for Shanks, and another would surely have ruined the record. But having lost Jim Given two minutes into the second half—Jim was sent off for a foul on Kidd—Clydebank were under heavy pressure. As ever, Hearts didn't even consider surrender—and Sandy Clark equalised from a MacDonald pass. Time: 86 minutes!

Clydebank:	Gallacher: Dickson, Given, Fallon, Auld, Treanor, Shanks, Gibson, Larnach, Maher (sub 49 mins), Lloyd, McCabe.
Hearts:	Smith: Kidd, Black, S. Jardine, Berry, MacDonald, Colquhoun, I. Jardine, McAdam (sub 45 mins), Clark, Mackay, Robertson.
Referee:	I. Cathcart, Bridge of Allan.

117

It's a quarter of a century since Hearts brought out a record of the most famous club song of them all. Namely of course: *Hearts, Hearts, Glorious Hearts!* It was sung by Hector Nicol and sold quite well. Obviously, it would have topped the charts, had not somebody decided to have the Hibs chant on the "B" side. This is rather like having Sidney Devine on the flip side of Sinatra. The story, as they prepare to play Dundee, is that Hearts will re-issue the record with, having no choice, a different singer.

Hearts 3 Dundee 1
8 February 1986

Hearts seem to be making a habit of giving the other lot a start. All's well that ends well, as they say, but most supporters would probably have preferred an end to such generosity. Dundee were the latest beneficiaries.

It's only fair to say, however, that the Dens team did look smart enough for an opening spell. They may even have merited their tenth-minute goal. But Henry Smith couldn't have been too pleased with himself. His colleagues were not noticeably delighted, either, when he dropped the ball on the six-yard line. Mennie was there.

But not even Henry is infallible. And if a goalie has an occasional lapse, it is up to the others to put it right. Which is what Hearts did, and before long. True, they wasted a penalty chance—John Colquhoun hit the ball weakly at Geddes—but after 22 minutes they were level. This time, Colquhoun didn't mess about.

Dundee were in trouble for most of the second-half, and an elegant passing move involving Whittaker, Colquhoun and Robertson was satisfactorily finished off . . . by Robertson. That was on the hour and eight minutes later Mackay beat three defenders including the goalkeeper, for the third.

Hearts:	Smith: Kidd, Black, S. Jardine, Berry, MacDonald, Colquhoun, Whittaker, Clark, Mackay, Robertson.
Dundee:	Geddes: Glennie, McKinlay, Forsyth, Smith, Duffy, Hendry, Brown, Mennie, Connor, Harvey.
Referee:	D. A. Yeats, Perth.

Celtic 1 Hearts 1
22 February 1986

Despite their position at the top of the League, despite the way they had achieved that lofty status, Hearts must still have been slightly surprised to know that they were betting favourites with the bookies for the Parkhead game. So far Celtic had not managed to win three consecutive matches. Hearts were going for their 20th league game in a row, undefeated.

But Celtic at Parkhead! And favourites! If that didn't confirm the status, what could have done? I cannot quite remember the odds against a draw, but I suppose they must have been 5-2 or a fraction better.

Henry Smith was an inspiration. One commentator, from Edinburgh, wrote that Henry had developed into one of the safest and steadiest goalkeepers in the land. The same fellow, unhappily, suggested that Celtic needed more players like Roy Aitken.

While it is true that Roy disturbed the smooth workings of the Hearts midfield, it is hardly credible that any really ambitious side could afford two like him. His dedication is absolute, his strength is frightening and I suppose I am about to fall into the trap of underrating the lad. But I honestly cannot see him as an integral part of a classic team. That said, if Hearts could ever afford him, that would be all right with me. So long as he was willing to learn.

Billy McKay, whose career with Rangers had seemed to be finished with a leg injury, was in the Hearts squad. He had called his signing by Hearts a new lease of life. He was to prove eminently worthy of it.

Anyway, this draw at Parkhead meant that Hearts had taken five points from Celtic during the season. Hearts weren't as good in the midfield as usual—give Roy Aitken more credit—and the defence seemed to be untypically vulnerable. In a match that took no prisoners and probably didn't inform the next-of-kin a point each seemed fair.

Celtic's goal came from a defensive mistake, but that kind of mistake usually occurs under pressure. Levein and Sandy Jardine were playing after-you-Claude, and Mo Johnston appeared on the scene to show how it should be done. That goal was scored after half-an-hour. But almost on half-time, Sandy Clark leaped to a lob from Ian Jardine and headed into the path of John Robertson. One each.

Celtic: Latchford: W. McStay, McGrain, Aitken, McCugan, MacLeod, McClair, McGhee, Shepherd (sub 74 mins), Johnston, Whyte, Burns.

Hearts: Smith: Kidd, Black, S. Jardine, Berry, Levein, Colquhoun, I. Jardine, Clark, G. Mackay, Robertson, W. McKay (sub 87 mins).

Referee: A. Ferguson, Giffnock.

Neil Berry in Cup Final action

Hamilton Accies 1 Hearts 2
Scottish Cup Fourth Round
3 March 1986

After four postponements we were beginning to wonder whether this tie would ever be played. From a neutral point of view, however, it was well worth waiting for. From a Hearts point of view, it might very well have shortened a few lives. To go out of the Scottish Cup is one thing ... to go out at the hands of a team from a lower division, however formidable, is quite another.

And that, as we all know, is something which we have suffered in the past. It didn't make sense that we should suffer it now! But Hearts had to fight very hard indeed, and it was just as well that they were good at overcoming adversity.

On a tight, treacherous pitch, Hamilton defended with courage and with excellent tactics—and were always liable to break dangerously. And yet again, Hearts lost an early goal. Correction: a very early goal. John Brogan needed half-a-minute to score after a nippy combination between Reid and McNaught.

John Robertson didn't need much time either—to equalise with a shot that went in off the post. Just as well John didn't hang about. The hearts of Hearts fans were beating somewhat too fast for their own health. Accies kept defending impressively until the 70th minute, when they had to give best to Gary Mackay, who swept in a pass from Robertson. Wee John's timing of the pass was perfect.

Hamilton:	Ferguson: Sinclair, Hamill, McNaught, Jamieson, Mitchell, Sprott, Clarke (sub 60 mins), Pelosi, Reid, O'Neill, Brogan.
Hearts:	Smith: Kidd, Black, S. Jardine, Berry, Levein, Colquhoun, Whittaker, Clark, G. Mackay, Robertson.
Referee:	B. McGinlay, Balfron.

Between the last match and the Scottish Cup-tie against St Mirren, Hearts fans had a few other topics of conversation. John Colquhoun fulfilled a lifetime ambition—his life to that point, of course—by meeting Neil Kinnock, in Scotland for the Labour

Party Conference in Perth. The meeting was arranged by the *Daily Record* and it was quite enjoyable to see John and Neil indulging in a game of head-tennis in the City Mills Hotel car park. With reluctance, having watched it all, I must confess that Neil, although greatly enthusiastic, would be better to stick to rugby.

Hearts 4 St Mirren 1
Scottish Cup quarter-final
9 March 1986

The score-line does, you have to admit, make it look so easy. In fact, it was easy in the end . . . but there were circumstances outside the control of St Mirren which made it so.

I do not believe that any Hearts fan—so long as he believes in the game itself—would argue about that. Within four minutes the Paisley goalkeeper, Campbell Money, jumped to grasp a so-called pass-back. He was challenged by Sandy Clark. All goalkeepers within range are challenged by Sandy Clark at all times. There was no suggestion of a foul. To the best of my knowledge, not even Campbell suggested as much later. But he still went down in a heap. The referee, quite rightly, delayed play for more than five minutes to allow Campbell the appropriate treatment. When this kind of thing happens, a goalkeeper is entitled to special, as well as appropriate, treatment.

The goalie came back, but looked like a well-refreshed punter leaving the Diggers at closing-time. Inevitably, Hearts attacked exuberantly. One St Mirren defender, who need not be named here—it was Neil Cooper, as far as I remember—indulged Campbell Money with yet another dodgy pass-back. Gary Mackay got there first, being easy favourite to do so, and touched it sideways to John Colquhoun, who scored. Meanwhile poor old Money was wondering whether it was Saturday, Sunday or Christmas. He was led away to hospital.

There was no valid competition after that. The only wonder is that Hearts scored only three more. Robertson headed into an empty net just on half-time. Cooper, who had volunteered to take over in goal, might as well have been playing brag on the terracing. He probably didn't notice Kenny Black's deflected goal early in the second-half, and didn't fancy himself—rightly so—with a John Robertson penalty kick that followed soon after.

McGarvey scored St Mirren's only goal on the hour, when Henry Smith was still feeling sorry for Campbell Money. The only other talking-point was the booking of John Colquhoun, who was carried off after being hit comprehensively by Steve Clarke. The referee, Mr Valentine, doubtless knew what that was all about. I didn't.

Hearts:	Smith: Kidd, Whittaker, S. Jardine, R. MacDonald (sub 75 mins), Berry, Levein, Colquhoun, W. McKay (sub 67 mins), Black, Clark, Mackay, Robertson.
St Mirren:	Money: Winnie (sub, but not in goal, 10 mins), Wilson, Abercromby, Rooney (75 mins), Cooper, Godfrey, Clarke, Fitzpatrick, Mackie, McGarvey, Gallacher, Spiers.
Referee:	R. Valentine, Dundee.

Hearts 2 Motherwell 0
15 March 1986

Now the Premier League record is equalled . . . the record of 21 consecutive matches without defeat . . . the record previously held by Rangers, who will presumably be hoping, via Graeme Souness, to do quite a bit better in season 1986-87. I'd advise you, however not to bet on that. Not just yet.

Hearts have 39 points from 29 games. Dundee United 36 from 28. Aberdeen 35 from 28. Celtic 33 from 27. Yes, Celtic, of course. Who can forget Celtic? But never mind that for now.

Motherwell began with a defiant zest. It was the defiance expected of a team that expects nothing. Hearts simply absorbed this initial pressure with a confidence that never descended to complacency. There was no real problem . . . although Motherwell, it is worth recalling, had just disposed of Dundee United. Motherwell's packed defence broke after half-an-hour, when Roddy MacDonald headed in a corner-kick. Ten minutes or so later Colquhoun was put on his backside in the box and Robertson scored simply enough. For Hearts the rest of the match was relaxation. Not for the first time, we wish they had knocked in quite a few more.

Hearts: Smith: Kidd, Whittaker, MacDonald, Berry, Levein, Colquhoun, Black, Clark, G. Mackay, Robertson, W. McKay (sub 58 mins).

Motherwell: Gardiner: Wishart, Murray, Doyle, Forbes, Boyd, Baptie, Macleod, Reilly, Wright, Blair (sub 55 mins), Walker.

Referee: D. Syme, Rutherglen.

Hibs 1 Hearts 2
22 March 1986

Always a big one. This time, bigger than ever. Hearts are storming towards the record of consecutive, undefeated Premier League matches. Not merely holding the record, note. *Breaking* it!

And against, of all clubs, Hibs! As the old cliché has it, you could have submitted the plot to any publisher—or even to TV, for goodness sake—and it would have been turned down as too fanciful. But that's the way it works out, and, in all honesty, if any Hearts punter tells me that he wasn't anxious before the game, I won't believe him. There's an air of Murphy's Law about the occasion. That is, if something *can* go wrong, it *will* go wrong.

Well, Hearts made it all right because quality does tend to count when all things are said and done, and even when bottles are going. It was not, however, as easy as most of us thought it would be. Hibs always try a bit against Hearts. It is a matter of pride, I suppose, and we must never grudge them that. Doug Baillie wrote: "I know Hibs and Hearts were battling to see who would be king of the castle. They could surely have gone about it with more regard for each other's health."

Doug can talk! I don't remember him worrying about the health, ill or otherwise, of any opponents. Especially when he played for Rangers.

The spirit of Hibs, never quenched, kept the game fairly exciting for a while, against the organisation—and the individual talents—of Hearts. But Hearts had even more than organisation, discipline and talent. They had the legs to keep running when Hibs were, figuratively, pleading for mercy.

Kenny Black does a Hampden soft-shoe shuffle

Sandy Clark's goal for Hearts was the reward for his opportunism, his ability to see a chance out of nowhere. He scored after 38 minutes. Steve Cowan headed a lovely equaliser—a thing of beauty to the Hibbies, anyway—in the 63rd minute. But justice was served, if only by one goal, when two minutes later Milne stopped a John Robertson header with his hands. This is not permitted. Robertson took the penalty himself and that was that.

Hibs: Rough: Milne, Sneddon, May, Fulton, Hunter, Collins, Chisholm, Cowan, Durie, Harris (sub 53 mins), Tortolano.
Hearts: Smith: Kidd, Whittaker, S. Jardine, Berry, Levein, Colquhoun, Black, Clark, Mackay, Robertson.
Referee: J. Duncan, Gorebridge.

P.S. to the above: the *Evening News* reported that a spectator was taken out of the Hearts end, fighting so frantically that six coppers were needed. Well, it is widely accepted that the Hibbies put in volunteers in maroon scarves into the Hearts end. This is to lessen the image of Hearts. But what do they give these lads to drink?

P.P.S. That's the league record, if you didn't notice . . . 22 in a row.

Hearts 3 St Mirren 0
25 March 1986

This is a re-arranged league game and, really, something of a formality. Hearts, after an entirely predictable win, are five points ahead of Dundee United and, in all competitions, have not been beaten in 26 consecutive games.

They were not, though, at their best, The crowd of 13,287 was excellent for a midweek game, but Tynecastle seemed strangely subdued. It was as if nobody—including St Mirren—expected much of a challenge to Hearts. This was how it turned out.

Only for a short while did St Mirren play like a Premier League side. McGarvey headed over when he should have scored and Gallacher was even more inept soon afterwards. A curious thing about Gallacher . . . which Hearts fans have recognised.

Give him a hard chance and he is likely to hit the back of the net. Give him an easy one and he appears to be too busy wondering why he deserves it.

Meanwhile, Hearts were steadily slipping into a purposeful rhythm. Just before the break, Robertson made sure that a Levein header went in. Campbell Money kept the score down for as long as he could but was still partly to blame for the second goal, scored in the 70th minute by John Robertson . . . a cheeky back-heel, no less. Sandy Clark got the third almost at the end from a clever, in-swinging Black corner-kick.

Hearts:	Smith: Kidd, Whittaker, S. Jardine, Berry, Levein, Colquhoun, Black, Clark, G. Mackay, Robertson.
St Mirren	Money: D. Hamilton, Clarke, Rooney, Godfrey, Cooper, B. Hamilton, B. Winnie, McGarvey, Gallacher, Spiers.
Referee:	K. O'Donnell, Airdrie.

In the programme for that St Mirren game, the chairman, Wallace Mercer, explained to the fans why Hearts had agreed to permit the league game against Aberdeen—scheduled for Sunday, 20 April—to be televised live. He took the view that the club had legally binding commercial contracts with sponsors. If Hearts had refused to take part, he wrote, they could have been sued for damages.

Hearts 3 Rangers 1
29 March 1986

It is now becoming a rather cruel joke in Edinburgh . . . or, that is, in those areas of Edinburgh where class football is understood and appreciated. "If we keep on beating the Rangers," Hearts fans are saying, "we'll get them to keep." It is really a joke. The company laws do not allow such a thing. One suspects that Mr Lawrence Marlborough, who owns Rangers, would oppose it anyway.

But Rangers are still presenting a decreasing problem for Hearts. It's not that they're such a bad team. It's just that they're not very good. On this occasion, they were aggressive enough towards the end but the aggression was inspired more by hurt pride than by creative build-up.

John Robertson was first off the mark, and he needed only eight minutes to get there, pouncing on a chip from Kenny Black and lobbing over Walker's head. The referee, Mr Alexander, made some eccentric decisions. For instance, the 46th minute free-kick to Hearts that appeared to have been the other way round. Nevermind, the free-kick led to a handling offence. Robertson scored with the penalty and that gave him 18 goals for the season. No other Hearts forward had scored so many since the Premier League was born.

There was confusion over a Hearts substitution—Mackay by Ian Jardine—when Rangers were given a penalty. It was for a foul on McCoist by Clark, who, as ever, was covering the whole park. McCoist scored efficiently. Then Clark finished a superb move superbly in the last minute.

As Rangers have fans everywhere, not all of the 25,000 crowd was pleased by the outcome. That gate was still among Britain's top five for the day.

Hearts:	Smith: Kidd, Whittaker, S. Jardine, Berry, Levein, Cólquhoun, Black, Clark, Mackay, I. Jardine (sub 67 mins), Robertson.
Rangers:	Walker: Burns, Munro, McPherson, MacKinnon, Durrant, McMinn, Fraser, Fleck, Cooper (sub 81 mins), Bell, Russell (sub 73 mins), McCoist.
Referee:	H. Alexander, Kilmarnock.

Dundee United 0 Hearts 1
Scottish Cup semi-final
5 April 1986

Hearts are not exactly accustomed to the expansive acres of Hampden Park. This doesn't worry them too much. This game takes them into the Cup Final and they have played 28 games, overall, without defeat. In the Premier League, of course, the total is 24.

In many ways, this semi-final against Dundee United was just about the biggest challenge Hearts faced all season. We noted earlier how many big names, established names, appeared regularly on the Tannadice team sheet. Think of it . . . five of this

Colquhoun scores against Aberdeen

semi-final side were destined to be part of the 22-man squad for Mexico. They were always going to be difficult to beat. Not merely because they had so many fine players, but also because there was little chance of their being over-awed by the occasion.

The way it worked out, however, Hearts proved to have at least as much talent—and certainly weren't over-awed, either.

United were probably too cautious. They appeared to take their class rather too much for granted, regarding it as inevitable that things would be all right eventually. Hearts took them on in every department, caring nothing for reputations. Hearts, after all, had their own reputations to consider.

John Colquhoun scored a magnificent goal in the 13th minute. As Malpas and Narey tried to get close enough to tackle, he volleyed a poor clearance from Hegarty high into the roof of the net. It was a brilliantly taken goal, quite typical of the man.

Semi-finals seldom produce good football. There's so much

at stake. For there's nothing worse than to be beaten in a semi-final. But there was much football to admire at Hampden that afternoon.

Of course, United turned on the pressure in the second-half. We could have expected no less of them. Hearts expected it, that's for sure, and absorbed everything with a placid determination . . . while persistently threatening on the break. Colquhoun, by virtue of that goal—and of many other menacing moments—will go down as the man of the match. Henry Smith was an honourable runner-up.

Dundee United: Thomson: Malpas, Holt, Gough, Hegarty, Narey, Bannon, Redford, Kirkwood, Gallacher (sub 45 mins), Sturrock, Dodds.

Hearts: Smith: Kidd, Whittaker, S. Jardine, Berry, Levein, Colquhoun, Black, Clark, Mackay, I. Jardine (sub 79 mins), Robertson.

Referee: B. McGinlay, Balfron.

Dundee United 0 Hearts 3
12 April 1986

For some reason there was an aura of anti-climax about a league match that was still crucial to Hearts. Maybe it was the result of the Hampden semi-final. Whatever the reason, it did not seem that Hearts could lose. This can be said despite the statistical fact that Dundee United had not lost at home in the League for 18 months.

Then again, I could be speaking through hindsight. I could be placing the memory of three outstanding goals against judgement. I don't know. Does it matter?

The first goal was lavishly praised on TV—and so it should have been. (So should they all have been, come to that.) It came after 23 minutes. Levein crossed into the penalty area and Hegarty didn't do well with the clearance. From about 20 yards out, John Robertson hit a left-foot cracker that seemed to be still rising as it whipped past Thomson.

At the start of the second-half Henry Smith made a save which Jim McLean compared with the one made by Gordon

Banks from Pele in the 1970 World Cup Finals. A fair comparison. I don't know how Henry saw the drive from Malpas in time. It fairly streaked through a crowd of players. He still got there, and I doubt if he will ever equal that instant of genius as long as he lives. Then again, you never know.

The 58th-minute second goal was my favourite because of the way it was fashioned. Cowie headed the ball out of defence, on to Berry, who crossed to the far post. Who was there but little John Colquhoun, rising to head into the path of Sandy Clark? There was a beatific smile on Sandy's face as he scored. Did I say that was my favourite goal of the three? I did, didn't I? It doesn't seem right to choose, all the same. I mean, consider the third goal!

The home defence was all over the place in the 66th minute, when Colquhoun slotted a dream of a pass through to John Robertson. Lots of strikers are murdered by nerves in this situation. The goalie seems to turn into King Kong. Robertson went round Thomson as if he hadn't been there, and the third goal was in.

Dundee United: Thomson: Malpas, Holt, Gough, Hegarty, Narey, Bannon, Gallacher, Beedie, Sturrock, Dodds.

Hearts: Smith: Cowie, Whittaker, S. Jardine, Berry, Levein, Colquhoun, Black, Clark, Mackay, Robertson.

Referee: K. J. Hope, Clarkston.

Controversy cast a certain cloud over the first-ever televised league game in Scotland. It came at a time when Hearts were approaching their 26th unbeaten game in a row, and their 30th overall. But would the fans turn up? Could it be an unreal atmosphere? How would the players and the fans react to an occasion which, though historic, remained full of problems?

Hearts 1 Aberdeen 1
20 April 1986

At least one question was answered. Live TV might have kept some fans at home. But with an attendance of 19,047—on a day that started with rain—the loyalty of the Hearts supporters

Sandy climbs that Aberdeen mountain

could hardly be doubted. The vast majority wanted to be *there*!

At the end of the afternoon Hearts were three points away from the title . . . their first Premier League title, and their first Scottish championship for 26 years. It could have been so different—in more ways than one. For Hearts showed definite signs of nervousness. That was probably to be expected, given the lack of experience of most of the side. But it was worrying all the same.

Alex MacDonald gasped afterwards: "Somebody up there likes me. We came back from the dead. We almost blew it." And so they did.

But if the composure of Hearts deserted them in this game, their determination was never more impressive. On the day, Aberdeen played the better football, directed by John McMaster, but still managed only one goal—and that was a justifiably disputed penalty kick in the 72nd minute.

I didn't have a clear view from the stand. Later, watching on the box, I still couldn't be sure. Who handled? More importantly, who handled first? Jim Bett or Ian Jardine? Mr Valentine voted for Jardine, Peter Weir took the kick, and Henry Smith, while guessing the direction of the ball correctly, couldn't stop it.

That was when Tynecastle nerves should have given way to sheer panic. Nothing of the sort happened. I refer, of course, to the players, not to the spectators.

Hearts attacked with a new-found smoothness. Sandy Jardine cleared cleverly, lofting the ball into the box. Robertson, always tenacious, flustered McQueen—and Colquhoun was there to punish the defender's mistake. There were three minuts to go . . .

Hearts: Smith: Cowie, Whittaker, S. Jardine, Berry, Levein, Colquhoun, Black, Clark, Mackay, I. Jardine (sub 75 mins), Robertson.
Aberdeen: Gunn: McKimmie, McQueen, McMaster, McLeish, Miller, Hewitt, Mitchell, Bett, Weir, J. Miller.
Referee: R. Valentine, Dundee.

Hearts 1 Clydebank 0
26 April 1986

Celtic are now putting up an unexpected challenge and it is highly advisable that Hearts should get both points against the team anchored at the foot of the Premier League. It is also advisable that Hearts should knock in lots and lots of goals in order that any such challenge is reduced to anonymity. But it doesn't quite work that way. Anxiety showed through again in almost everything Hearts did.

Under no pressure—like Aberdeen the previous week—and knowing that relegation had been suspended, Clydebank were able to cause Hearts all kinds of trouble. They didn't score but Henry Smith had a fair bit to do with that. Of the strikers who had been so dangerous and so composed for the unbeaten run, only John Colquhoun looked really on top form, especially in the first-half. Possibly Gary Mackay was bearing that in mind when, in the 34th minute, he scored the goal that was to win the game.

Deceiving the defence with a swerving forward run, he hit a fine left-foot shot past Gallacher from outside the box.

Hearts seemed more like their old selves in the second-half, but there wasn't much wrong with the Clydebank defence. Moreover, Gerry McCabe was a constant nuisance . . . so much so that the feeling in the 21,000 crowd at the 90th minute was one of relief.

Hearts:	Smith: Cowie, Whittaker, S. Jardine, Berry, Levein, Colquhoun, Black, I. Jardine (sub 68 mins), Clark, Mackay, Robertson.
Clydebank:	Gallacher: Dickson, Given, Maher, Auld, Treanor, Shanks, Hughes, Moore (sub 70 mins), Bain, Conroy, McCabe.
Referee:	K. O'Donnell, Airdrie.

That's 50 points from 35 matches. A Premier League total of 27 unbeaten games in a row . . . far and away a record. An all-match total of 31 unbeaten. Now it's off to Dens Park for the crunch match of the season.

Neil Berry thunders the ball against the Aberdeen crossbar in the Cup Final

Crunch at Dens Park

IT'S THE MORNING of the last league game of the season, at Dundee, and I understand as well as anybody why Hearts fans will not care to be reminded of that day. But if we are talking about the season, it's not really too easy to leave it out. Much as one would like to do so.

At Tynecastle, there are queues round the block for Cup Final tickets. McLeod Street is a mess. Coaches manoeuvre delicately between the parked cars, and there's barely room for a bicycle. Other cars, even other coaches, persist in trying to get in from Gorgie Road. Tempers are being lost. It's only half-past-ten.

In the secretary's office, Pilmar Smith is fiddling, though with a certain expertise, with portable telephones. One goes to Paisley, the other goes to Dens Park. "Let's hope the score at Paisley doesn't matter," says Pilmar, "but we don't want to rely on crackling transistors." At this time, we're obviously still hoping that St Mirren will be putting up some sort of respectable opposition to Celtic.

Wallace Mercer arrives, looking worried. He says everybody else seems worried. He senses something and he isn't wrong. Pilmar tells him about Craig Levein, down with the virus that has been troubling several other Hearts men this week. For sound reasons it has been kept quiet. Wallace shakes his head. It's not that he doesn't have faith in, or respect for, big Roddy

MacDonald, the natural replacement, it's just that forebodings seem to be emphasised now. "I've hardly slept all week," he says.

"Join the club," I say.

"Let's get into the bus," says Wallace.

This is a good idea, or at least it would have been a good idea, only the bus isn't there and the traffic jam is worse. Wallace apologises to the lads in the ticket queue, and he means it, because they are customers and he doesn't like to see customers kept waiting. It's reckoned that 15,000 ground tickets had been sold the previous day. Now Wallace tells the fans that more are being sent through from Glasgow. We hear a horror story about the shrewd fellow who went through to the SFA headquarters at Park Gardens, asked for tickets and was asked, in turn, how many he wanted. He came back to Edinburgh, apparently, with 70 centre stand tickets.

There are, at this time, absolutely no stand tickets available at Tynecastle, the allocation having been pathetic . . . 1,500. Nor, of course, does Glasgow have a team in the final. We leave Tynecastle at about 11am, a bit late, but nobody is bothering. There's much admiration for the way the driver backs out into Gorgie Road. It is deserved.

Some players get involved in a card-game, for low stakes, and the others read the morning papers. There's an inevitable yet nagging unanimity about these morning papers. There seems no doubt that Hearts are destined to be champions. That sense of foreboding doesn't go away, and I do not write merely with the benefit of hindsight. It's as if it's all just too good to be true.

"We'll win by four," I tell Wallace, and he doesn't believe me any more than I believe myself.

And yet it's surely not just whistling in the dark. We know that Dundee are a formidable lot at Dens Park, and well worth watching anywhere else. They have a hoodoo, it seems, on Hearts. But the *Scotsman* says that "a feature of the Tynecastle side's run has been the ability to lay assorted bogeys". The *Daily Record* has the headline: "Hearts' Last Lap To Glory". "Within touching distance of the jackpot," says Jim Kean. The *Glasgow Herald* insists that it would take a perverse twist of fate to deny

Hearts, admits that this is possible, then adds that it is a long shot. At least 10-1, according to most bookmakers, and a bit more than that according to those few bookmakers willing to take a chance.

Then we note the other story in the *Daily Record*, the one about Alan Gordon, who played for Hearts when Kilmarnock won the League in 1965 in that awful game at Tynecastle. By scoring just one goal, Hearts could hardly have lost. But the word "Kilmarnock" is taboo. Or, at best, it is whispered.

Meanwhile, the directors are discussing how to fit folk into the élite seats at the Cup Final. "We've got to do it sometime," says Wallace Mercer, "so we might as well do it now." What he really means is that it helps to take his mind, temporarily, away from the events due later that day.

The discussion is all friendly, with big Douglas Park and Pilmar Smith expressing mock gratitude to Wallace. "Are you sure Pilmar and Bobby and me are allowed seats?" asks Douglas, and Wallace chuckles.

"This is very much a democracy," he tells me.

As a matter of fact, the workings of the Hearts board are a lot more democratic than you might expect in an organisation where one man has a major shareholding. Pilmar Smith is never loth to speak his mind. Douglas Park, a wealthy man in his own right, is not a man to cross lightly. And Bobby Parker, one of the great Hearts of the 1950s, while weighing his words, makes them tell.

At the Swallow Hotel, on the edge of Dundee, the players vanish to a private dining-room, for scrambled egg and not much else, and we adjourn to the bar. Wallace is on the bell. He has his critics but he is no piker. Everybody is remarkably abstemious, including me. I've been feeling like a large brandy, to settle the nerves, but I opt for a lager. Pilmar, who isn't very good at it, has a Perrier Water, which might as well come out of a tap. Les Porteous is happy with a white wine. I take the view that Wallace gets off lightly in the end.

I have no interest in lunch, and let the rest of them go. At the bar, I meet Jimmy McDowall, a 22-year-old knitwear worker from Glenrothes, and Alistair Bryce, a 21-year-old joiner from Edinburgh. They are typical of the decent young Hearts fans, of whom there are many thousands. But they are blatantly worried. The foreboding has got to them too. They have never seen Hearts win anything. They ask me questions about Willie Bauld and Jimmy Wardhaugh and Dave Mackay and John Cumming and Alex Young.

"We're going to do it, aren't we?" they then ask, as if I were an oracle.

"No danger," I say. What *else* can I say?

From the hotel to the ground, the atmosphere lightens. *The Hearts Song* blares out on the coach radio, the players join in. So does Wallace Mercer, although Wallace says he fancies himself as a Sinatra type. He also joins in the flip side, *New York, New York*. I suspect that he doesn't really mean this, even if the lyrics do include "king of the hill, top of the heap".

There are many Hearts colours to be seen on the way to Dens Park. There are no Dundee colours.

The coach drops the players at the front door and takes the directors down to the car park. Obviously, they want to let the players in first and, anyway, there's plenty of time. Walking back, Wallace is spotted by a crowd of Hearts supporters who follow him, chanting, "Jesus, Jesus, give us a wave". This is possibly somewhat blasphemous, but it is intended to recognise the fact that he was something of a messiah when he first arrived at Tynecastle. He takes it well enough. He is used to it. The lyrics improve, as the game is about to start—"Only One Wallace Mercer".

"Stop blushing," I tell him. "You deserve it." And he does.

Soon after, I'm looking across at big Doug Baillie, who is in the press box. Doug was a substantial centre-half for Rangers and Dunfermline. Now he writes entertainingly for the *Sunday Post*. He is in contact with Paisley as fast as the mobile phones. He keeps indicating the score, and it's looking bad.

Of course, the score at Love Street wouldn't matter if Hearts were doing the business at Dens, but that is palpably what they are not doing. True, they looked slightly promising in the first

Sandy Clark is foiled by the goalkeeper against Dundee

half-hour, but slight promises do not win titles. The virus clearly has something to do with a strange sort of lethargy which seems to be affecting Hearts players . . . or some of them at any rate. Roddy MacDonald, taking Craig Levein's place, is outstanding, and he has to be. So is Neil Berry. Sandy Jardine tries to keep himself and everybody else cool by example. But there is too much pressure from Dundee. It isn't that Hearts are playing a deliberate policy of deep defence. It's just that things are working out that way, whether Hearts like it or not.

We have not lost faith yet, but the nerves are certainly jangling. Whenever Dundee cross the half-way line, which is far too frequently, the tension on the terraces can almost be touched. Those who for most of the season have admired the skilful and creative build-up by Hearts, now feel mightily relieved by punts upfield. Anything to get the ball away from the Hearts goal. It looks like a penalty when Sandy Clark is brought down, but the referee doesn't think so. Too much reliance is being placed on

Clark, one feels. Too many passes aimed hopefully in his direction. He's a valuable player, is Sandy, but the Dundee defenders are as tall as he is and Jim Duffy is strolling around as if he owned the park. John Colquhoun does his best, as ever, but isn't getting the service, and he is slowing down. What has happened to John Robertson? He is hardly noticed. Gary Mackay is making no impact, either, and Ian Jardine looks dreadfully tired. We hear later that he has been injured.

And yet, despite a general display which bears no resemblance to those which set up that league record, the minutes are passing ever more quickly, it seems, and maybe we're going to do it, after all.

There are only seven minutes, seven measly miserable little minutes, when Albert Kidd hooks a shot out of a scramble and into the Hearts net. All the premonitions of the day now emphasise reality.

We are beaten, we have lost the game, we have lost the title.

The second goal for Dundee, also by Kidd, is about as useful as an ash-tray on a motor-bike, or even a chocolate teapot. Such figures of speech may not be original, but I'm not apologising for that. That first goal is the goal that matters and all that we have feared has come to pass.

Alex Ferguson, who has been at Dens in order to see how best his Aberdeen side can take on Hearts in the Scottish Cup Final, has left, without seeing a goal.

At the full-time whistle, at the end of all this trauma, at the final trumpet, the only emotion left is drained, stunned despair. The fact that we had, perversely, thought it might happen anyway, didn't matter any more. Some Hearts fans weep. They should not be ashamed. There is nothing wrong with honest emotion. There is nothing wrong with giving way, after a day of exceptional ambition, to the realisation that the dream is shattered.

Somehow, Celtic have scored five goals against St Mirren. It is a score which pays tribute to the tenacity of the Glasgow club but which pays no tribute whatsoever to the attitude of St Mirren. You could have had long-odds against Celtic for the title in the morning. You could have named your own odds against a 5-0 score.

It was 4-0 for Celtic at half-time, and, in the directors' lounge, somebody said that St Mirren did not seem to be knocking their pans in, as the saying goes. I have no way, at this time, of knowing what the Hearts fans on the terracing were saying, courtesy of these crackling transistor radios, about St Mirren. This is possibly just as well.

It is now time for a confession, of a kind.

Just before Dundee scored their first goal, I had left the immediate premises. I was downstairs in the lounge, watching television but not actually seeing television. I am convinced that most Hearts fans would have been pleased to leave around that time. If you have not experienced such anxiety, then there's nothing I can tell you, but I suspect I will be easily understood.

Listen, I remember how the incomparable Jim Baxter left his seat at Ibrox—he had been injured and couldn't play—and paced around the front of the grandstand when Hearts were one up by a Donald Ford goal. That day Hearts won, by the way.

Be that as it may, at least I had somewhere to go. For the first time in my life, I had been invited to the directors' box, and football club directors are well treated. Which is why I moved downstairs to the lounge where, at half-time, a man could have lived for two days on the spread laid out ... everything from nice wee hot pies to Scotch eggs to delicate salmon sandwiches.

At half-past-four that afternoon, I felt heart-sorry for the fans who had nowhere to go, but who had to stick it out. I say this because I cannot doubt that they, too, were concerned to the point of terror. How many nails were bitten to the knuckle before Dundee scored? How many brave hearts were strained to the utmost before Dundee scored yet again? And when that happened, how many of the boys were trying to get out while attempting not to let anybody see the tears?

You see, it's all very well to talk about football being only a game. In the most literal of terms, it is probably just that. Only a game?

In the hearts and souls and minds of thousands, of millions, it is one hell of a lot more than a game. For God's sake, rugby is a game, cricket is a game. There are even those who say that the pastimes of snooker and darts constitute a version of sport. To put football in such categories is to lose the entire meaning of it. Football is so much more than a game. Football is a way of life, a cherished thread of existence, for so many.

When the thread breaks, even if its renewal is inevitable, people do cry.

Only twice have I felt the lump in the throat, the tears welling up, in this game of football. The first time was when Hibs beat Hearts 7-0, and I do not forget how luckily they achieved such a result. That superb journalist, Hughie Taylor, saw me in the old Hearts Club, and suggested that I was denigrating the profession. He was probably right. John Barleycorn had something to do with it, too, as Hugh may agree. He's not exactly teetotal himself, not the last time I saw him, anyway. Although, at his age, he damned well should be.

The second time I blinked away tears, in a similar context . . . I'll tell you about that later.

The game is lost, the title is lost, and downstairs Alex Kitson, the trade unionist and staunch Hearts supporter, tries courageously to put things into perspective. He talks about winning and losing, about all sorts of philosophical attitudes. Alex is the former number two in the TGWU and, as a power-broker, he was on his own. He used to be Sean Connery's boss, in the milkman days of 007, and he is assuredly a Hearts man. But when he tries to tell me about taking it easy, I remember how he was in that very directors' box. He was leaping about like a prawn in a hot frying-pan, and I'm still not too pleased about the things he was calling the referee. Then again, considering that I agreed with him at the time, and especially over the issue of that aborted penalty, I may not be especially well-qualified to judge.

David Scott, now controller of news and current affairs on Scottish Television, is feeling a bit better now, possibly because of the glasses of Hundred Pipers laid out in the lounge. So am I. (Incidentally, if there are any Hearts fans who think less of me for indulging in the odd free refreshment, I'll tell them now that

I much prefer the Diggers, Mathers, the Gordon Arms and the Murrayfield Bar. There are, after all, things that one must do in the cause of duty.)

David tells Wallace Mercer that he won't be crying any more that day, having come to terms with the situation. There's no way of knowing whether David can fulfil that promise. His eyes still look red.

The Dundee chairman makes a small speech. It's something about how he thought Rangers were only drawing at Motherwell. This, we assume, is supposed to be some kind of apology for the jubilation he showed over the Dens result. Dundee, as will be recalled, would have won a place in Europe, had Rangers indeed got no more than one point. Anyway, we believe Mr Gellatly.

Just as we believe the Dundee manager, Archie Knox, when he says that he is as sad as Alex MacDonald over the result. Archie, consigned to the directors' box during a game because of his exuberance, has spent that match trying to take bites out of

John Robertson tries to control the traffic against Dundee

143

the walkie-talkie linked to the dug-out. We still believe him and we still appreciate his sympathy, more or less.

Outside Dens Park, the players and the directors are cheered on their way to the team bus. This is a sign of the sportsmanship of the Hearts supporters, many of whom have been clamouring for the players outside the dressing-room.

There's supposed to be a police escort to the motorway, or anyway out of the Dundee city boundary. This makes me feel important. I've never before been in a coach with a police escort. The initial experience, may I say, is not worth remembering. The police car merely took up space. The coppers clearly support Dundee, Celtic or St Mirren. We progress at snail's pace.

On the bus, the players sit at the back and they are not so much subdued as desolate. You could have brought a circus elephant, complete with funny hat, on to the bus and they wouldn't have looked up.

Wallace Mercer talks about the Rudyard Kipling poem, *If*. It's the one about treating these two impostors, triumph and disaster, the same. He tells Bobby Parker that Bobby can now wear a different suit. Bobby, who has worn the same suit since Hearts started their record-breaking run—it's an unusual shade of brown, I'd say—nods sadly.

We pass supporters' buses on their way home. Incredibly, they wave and cheer as we pass. They could not have been more enthusiastic had we won the game. They even blow kisses. They are young lads for the most part and all they know about the history of Hearts is what they have been told by their fathers and grandfathers.

At Tynecastle, a sizeable crowd waits to welcome the bus. That's when the lump in the throat assumes embarrassing proportions. I'm looking for a pint in the Tynecastle Arms, but it's packed. At the Press Club, a good friend, well-oiled by his own admission, says he will lay 25-1 against Hearts for the Cup. He is really sick. He says he'll never go back.

Big Gus Young, the photographer, says it was the worst day of his life. I walk home, stop in at Mathers at the West End, and another friend, although a Hibbie, tells me that he is far from unhappy about what has happened. Somehow I respect that.

The rivalry between Hearts and Hibs is healthy enough. It becomes unhealthy and offensive only when religion, or pseudo-religion, is introduced.

No true Hearts fan would wish Hibs to be relegated. It is a pleasant thought that we can play them four times a year and be reasonably sure of, say, half-a-dozen League points. The worst sort of Hibs supporter is the one who says he wants Hearts to win the League, if Hibs can't win it. He is lying in his teeth. He is a hypocrite.

This is what we have to tolerate for days after the defeat at Dens Park. It would be hard to keep one's temper, but for another statistic—the one that shows the Hibernian Football Club to be third from the bottom.

Next season, we know only too well, circumstances could be reversed. That's all right if that's what is decreed. All my Hibbie friends—and you'd be astonished how many I have—will know that I wish them all the best. Correction: second-best.

But it was still a bad day at Dens, wasn't it?

Dundee:	Geddes: Smith, McCormack (Sub 76 mins), Hendry, Duffy, Glennie, Shannon, Brown, Connor, McKinlay, Kidd (sub 61 mins), Nebbie, Harvey.
Hearts:	Smith: Kidd, S. Jardine, R. MacDonald, Whittaker, Black (sub 54 mins), I. Jardine, W. Mackay (sub 85 mins), Berry, G. Mackay, Colquhoun, Clark, Robertson.
Referee:	W. Crombie, Edinburgh.

Manager Alex MacDonald greets the fans at Hampden

The Hampden Showdown

ON THE MORNING of the 1985-86 Scottish Cup Final at Hampden, Saturday 10 May, somebody said that the previous week had been like the week between Christmas and New Year. I suppose the big difference was that there hadn't been much to celebrate or to sing carols about at Dens, but it was well put.

It did seem like an unreal time, a limbo time. For most Hearts fans the stunning disappointment of losing the championship didn't wear off until Tuesday or Wednesday. And there was a persistent feeling of disbelief. But then we started consoling ourselves with the thought that few teams would have been given, so quickly, a second chance for a major honour.

And so we actually began looking forward to the Cup Final. Wallace Mercer told the press: "My concern now is to lift everyone from despair. On Saturday we have the chance to bounce back and give our super fans the victory they want."

"We face a character test now," said Sandy Jardine on the Tuesday.

Meanwhile it was revealed the stomach virus had affected Craig Levein, Brian Whittaker, John Colquhoun, Kenny Black, John Robertson and Neil Berry. Obviously that had had a debilitating affect on the play at Dundee, but at the same time nobody was making any excuses. It was more a question of crossing fingers and hoping that there would be at least eleven fit men available for Hampden.

It was on the Wednesday that Alex Ferguson released an item of news which did the morale of Hearts no harm. The Aberdeen manager withdrew Eric Black from his Cup Final pool as a punishment for Black's deal with the French club, Metz. Black's contract was about to expire, but Ferguson was also giving his opinion of agents who "tap" star players. Well, we thought to ourselves, if Aberdeen don't play a scoring-machine like Black, that's all right with us.

Then Ian Jardine fell victim to the dreaded bug and the Black story didn't matter so much.

One thing not affected was the sale of tickets for the final. It was estimated that 35,000 Hearts fans would be making their way to Hampden on the big day. The figure turned out to be nearer 40,000. And on the Friday the *Daily Record* came out with a fascinating tale about Sandy Jardine. "I joined Rangers as a striker originally," said Sandy, "and I was on the substitute's bench for the Celtic-Rangers Cup Final 17 years ago. We were hammered 4-0, but do you remember who was playing centre for Rangers that day? Alex Ferguson, that's who. Davie White had to choose between Alex and me . . . I think he picked Alex because his elbows were sharper."

It was encouraging to find on the Saturday morning that most of the newspapers were tipping Aberdeen. That, at any rate, was what we told ourselves. Maybe we needed all the encouragement we could get, false or otherwise.

Determined to finish the season in some kind of style, whatever the result, I was in the Sheraton at half-past-ten in the morning on Cup Final Day, quaffing champagne with the Hearts' Executive Club. Quite rapidly I worked it out that this was an excellent way to start any day, if you can get away with it, and I was in good company.

The irrepressible Nancy Hogg, who supervises the Executive Club's room on match days, distributed song-sheets on the bus to Glasgow. Some sang, some didn't. Despite the lavish rations of bubbly previously dispensed, I confess I wasn't in great voice. It seemed a better idea to wait until the return journey.

Andy Cameron, Jimmy Bone and Willie "Bud" Johnston

Robertson chips over Leighton–and just over the crossbar

joined us for lunch at the Albany, and Jimmy was especially cheerful. "Don't worry," he said, "Hearts will do it. They've got it here, where it counts." And he patted his chest. Jimmy always did have lots of heart himself and his prophecy seemed sound. "Bud" sipped cola, and wondered if the mysterious virus had had anything to do with sheer nerves. And he reminisced: "You know something, I was thinking of buying Hearts once. Honest. It was, oh, six or seven years ago, and they were in deep trouble, but I always knew the potential support was there. We were in the Ibrox dressing-room, and I said to Sandy Jardine and Alex Miller that if we could raise fifty grand each, it could be a great investment. But maybe it's just as well that Wallace beat us to it. . ."

Jimmy Bone, now managing Arbroath, spoke of the "cool dudes" in football. "They're the kind of players who are more likely to be dripping gold than sweat. Hearts haven't got any like that, thank goodness." One had the suspicion that any cool dudes at Arbroath wouldn't last long, either.

Andy Cameron was in his usual fine form. He recalled the Rangers annual general meeting, at which he had advocated a relaxation, shall we say, in the Ibrox recruitment policy. "I thought I'd get a bit of stick for that," he said, "but at the next game it looked as if I was going to survive. Then somebody asked me for my autograph and there was this voice roaring from a few rows back in the stand, 'Hey, Cameron, dinna sign your name, just rattle your beads'. And that was my brother, tae."

"Oh yes," he said, "you know this big wedding, the royal wedding, on the twenty-third of July? Well, they were going to have it on the twelfth, but they couldnae get a band."

On the coach from the hotel to Hampden, I drew Henry Smith in the first-to-score sweep. I restrained myself from demanding a stewards' inquiry. How can you put goalkeepers in a sweep when they don't even take penalties? Anyway, I didn't think it was a very good omen.

But then we had reached that stage of the day where good or bad omens can be spotted all over the place. On the coach radio, The Stones sang *This could be the last time*. One line leapt out from another song . . . "You had your chance, and you blew it".

The traffic certainly took the Glasgow police by surprise. Maybe they're not accustomed to handling big crowds. We just made it for the kick-off, a mixed blessing. A few minutes later and we might have missed Aberdeen's first goal. It has to be admitted, though, that the goal was worth seeing, even if it did go into the wrong net. The Hearts defence didn't seem to have settled down at all, and Hewitt should probably have been tackled before cracking in a low fierce drive that would have beaten any goalkeeper.

Some reports suggested the following morning that this goal knocked the heart out of Hearts. I suggest, in turn—and I'll be backed by the enormous Hearts contingent in the 62,841 crowd—that it did nothing of the sort. In fact Hearts commanded most of the play and created by far the more chances in the rest of the half. Neil Berry was immense as Hearts kept the midfield. But what Hearts couldn't do was turn the expertly organised Dons defence. Gary Mackay caused them plenty of trouble, even

Captain Kidd surges through in attack at Hampden

moments of near-panic, and so did John Colquhoun. But Gary especially, while brave and showing all the skills we know he has, was too apt to delay his shot. He still gave John Robertson a chance at an open goal, but wee John was untypically hesitant. Perhaps he was put off by the inevitable Aberdeen appeals for offside.

A quick goal at the start of the second-half would not only have made a tremendous difference to Hearts. It would also have been well deserved. But in the 48th minute it was Aberdeen who scored again. Weir was giving Kidd a difficult afternoon and from his cross, dummied by McDougall, Hewitt whipped the ball in from close range. Still Hearts showed no sign of surrender. Berry hit the crossbar and there might easily have been a penalty when Kidd was sent crashing down in the box.

Aberdeen's third goal, a beautifully timed header from Stark, finished the match as a contest, if not as a topic for debate.

Aberdeen's constant niggling and gamesmanship, unworthy of a side with so many fine players, caused Hearts increasing

151

frustration and, in all honesty, I cannot blame them. I wrote on the Sunday morning that Aberdeen were almost a replica of the Leeds United side which, under Don Revie, were the most efficient and also the most unpopular in England some 16 years ago. This Cup Final emphasised the tendency of Willie Miller and Alex McLeish to usurp the role of referee. That should not be interpreted as special criticism of the referee, Hugh Alexander. He is but one of many other referees who have failed to tell Willie and Alex to get on with the game and stop laying down the laws. But the Aberdeen tactics help to explain an astonishing statistic. Three Hearts men were booked—Berry, Robertson and Mackay—and Kidd was sent off midway through the second-half. And how many Aberdeen players fell foul of the referee? Actually, none.

That said, however, I must stress that there can be no denying the power and skills of Aberdeen. They proved themselves to be the better team on the day, even if the score-line exaggerated the extent of their victory.

Hearts:	Smith: Kidd, Whittaker, S. Jardine, Berry, Levein, Colquhoun, Black, Clark, Mackay, Robertson.
Aberdeen:	Leighton: McKimmie, McQueen, McMaster, Stark (sub), McLeish, W. Miller, Hewitt, J Miller (sub), Cooper, McDougall, Bett, Weir.
Referee:	Hugh Alexander, Kilmarnock.

On the homeward journey, we did not know that Alex Ferguson, in the ritual after-the-match comments, had said: "Even though we won, this season has belonged to Hearts. I'm as sick as anybody that they didn't get the trophy they deserved." Had we known, of course, this would have cheered us up greatly. After we had worked out to which trophy Alex was referring.

But that's by the way. Nancy was still asking if we were down-hearted—a few liars and closet-Hibbies answered in the negative—and now she was threatening to fine all non-singers a fiver. I managed a few lines of *The Hearts Song* and *Flower of Scotland*, but I wasn't giving Kenneth McKellar anything to worry about.

Nobody volunteered to sing *The Northern Lights*.

The day, as we all now know, wasn't over. Far from it. Only the coldest and least romantic of folk could have failed to be moved by the incredible acclaim for the players as their coach arrived for a reception at the Caledonian Hotel soon after eight o'clock. The crowd was estimated at well over 3,000, and many of these fans had arrived an hour previously. They sang a lot, and some cried a little. But they were there.

The Edinburgh police, with rather more perception than their Glasgow colleagues, were all geared up for the occasion, although some of the mounties didn't look too comfortably seated when the lads arrived, to a crescendo of cheering.

I heard one maroon-bedecked fan remark, with a certain bitterness, that Aberdeen wouldn't attract as many people when they came home *with* the cup. I suspect he wasn't entirely correct in that assumption, but I do remember that when the Aberdeen followers sang *The Northern Lights* at the end of the match at Hampden, they could have been drowned out by a Brownie choir in top form. So he might have had a point at that.

As at Hampden, the fans at the Caledonian Hotel stayed long after the main event. The players had gone inside, all emotionally wrecked, a few—like those so-talented youngsters, Gary Mackay and John Robertson—quite visibly so. But as if in defiance of such things as results, these fans, these remarkable fans, continued for at least an hour to chorus a gratitude which was not misplaced.

In the Press Club, a few doors from the hotel, Davie Mowat, the manager, was bearing up well after one of the biggest disappointments of his life. Harry West inadvertently put soda in my Laphroaig, and I stopped remonstrating with him after only two minutes. Big Gus Young, who is to be seen regularly at Tynecastle behind the goal with his camera, eventually cheered up too. Paul Clancy, who had been sicker than the proverbial parrot after the Dens Park job—like vowing never to go back— was saying how proud he was to be a Hearts supporter. Young Norrie Stewart was trying to find a tape of *The Hearts Song* for the club record-player. He couldn't find the tape, so we sang the song instead. After seeing the Caledonian welcome, it seemed the only thing to do.

The Secret of Success

IT IS UNLIKELY that any club will ever again build up a record of 27 consecutive unbeaten League games—plus four more in the Scottish Cup—and have nothing tangible to show for it.

Certainly we wouldn't wish it on any other club.

But this is a good time to get things into a sensible perspective. There is no point in talking any more about what might have been. Let's look at the positive achievements up to now . . . and at the feasibility of achieving plenty in the future.

Some months ago, Alex MacDonald said that he was aiming for a league place worth European competition next season and for a good run in the Scottish Cup. These aims have been achieved. They have come very close indeed to being surpassed—spectacularly.

Hearts, always a big club, are now once again *recognised* as such. Hearts are respected not only in Scottish football but throughout European football. Anyone who doubts this should have been in Les Porteous's office when foreign journalists were seeking accreditation, and in the boardroom when Wallace Mercer was speaking to Continental TV stations. One phrase was frequently used about Hearts as the team was amassing that total of undefeated matches. The sleeping giant! Well, the giant is now very much awake. It won't go to sleep again.

There cannot be any question about who set off the alarm clock.

Five years ago, and this is an oft-told tale, Hearts were in serious danger of extinction. The decline had entered on the slippiest of financial slopes since that appalling game against Kilmarnock in the spring of 1965: the game in which Hearts lost the title by a fraction of goal-average. If they had lost it well, the reaction among the fans might not have been so drastic. They lost it badly. They lost it without regard for the great Tynecastle tradition which insists on real football.

And so Hearts were virtually up for sale. But who wanted to buy a football club deep in debt and with, apparently, scant prospect of getting out of it?

Two people, as it turned out. One was Kenny Waugh, who later took over Hibs, for his sins. The other was Wallace Mercer, who won that particular duel comfortably enough with an investment of £400,000 to become principal shareholder. And, not long after, chairman.

From the moment Wallace Mercer moved in, the bad old ideas moved out.

He realised, above all, that a football club is part of a community, and that it needs community support. This inspired a view of public relations which would have horrified the Tynecastle régime of not so very long ago. In essence, he wanted the public in general, and Hearts supporters specifically, to understand that the club was theirs.

Quite deliberately, he gave himself a high media profile. A reporter could call him at just about any time, in his office or at home. He was always willing to talk, always ready with an opinion. And still is.

In the last couple of years, this policy has provoked envy, even resentment, within the crustier corners of the football establishment. You could almost hear the old gentlemen—some from clubs that couldn't equal one Hearts' gate over a whole season—asking each other, querulously: "Who is this upstart Mercer, anyway?" None of that seemed to bother him.

Hearts became the subject of so many headlines that even Celtic and Rangers were beginning to wonder where they were going wrong. Hibs were notably disturbed. That didn't bother him either.

But it was no cynical exercise on behalf of Wallace Mercer. It was a genuine and successful attempt to regain a place for Hearts in the minds of anybody ever thinking of going back to football. Or to Tynecastle anyway.

If I hear an accusation of cynicism, I tell the accuser about the morning of the crunch league game at Dens Park, when Wallace Mercer, having just heard the news of Craig Levein's illness, earnestly discussed—on the McLeod Street pavements—Hearts' chances with a couple of kids neither of whom was more than fourteen. I can think of no other football club chairman, past or present, who would have done that. Can you?

Wallace is 39-years-old and has described himself as an "overweight little man, at 14½ stone and 5 feet 9 inches". I suppose he *is* overweight, judging by these statistics, but it doesn't affect his energy. Maybe if he didn't drink gassy, bottled beer he could get rid of a few pounds, but who am I to talk?

He was born in Dunoon and brought up in Glasgow. He was ten when his father, a tax-man, died, and he remembers no silver spoon in those days. At 18, he left home for a job with a paper-making firm in London—"and I studied business management whenever I could". Married at 21, he scraped enough to buy a house, sold it at a reasonable profit—the first of plenty—and returned north. The profit was enough for a stake in the property game. Now he is managing director of a highly successful property group, which is linked to a long-established insurance institution.

If anybody can be called Mr Hearts, that man is Wallace Mercer.

He picks people well. He is responsible for the management team of Alex MacDonald and Sandy Jardine, and if he never does anything else for Hearts, he will be remembered for that alone.

Alex MacDonald is Manager of the Year. Sandy Jardine is Player of the Year. Hearts supporters were delighted to hear that Rangers had appointed Graeme Souness as manager. They had feared, and probably with reason, that Rangers might have poached MacDonald and Jardine. That would have been a cruel blow because if there is any secret in the way Hearts raced to a

Premier League record, it is in the minds of these two, with the coach, Walter Borthwick, adding the benefits of his own considerable experience.

In fact, there is probably no secret as such. Hearts have a blend of youth and experience. That's hardly a secret. They are exceptionally fit. That's the result of sensible training methods—none of them a secret—allied to the sprinting techniques taught by George McNeill, the fastest Briton in the history of athletics, amateur or professional. But George doesn't shroud his techniques in mystery. Many pros use them. And yet . . . this Hearts team has several players not regarded as good enough by their former clubs. How did they succeed so dramatically at Tynecastle? Partly because Alex and Sandy spotted qualities which those other clubs had simply not exploited. Mainly, however, because of the atmosphere at Tynecastle.

It is a happy place. Players like coming in to work. They don't look on it as work anyway. There are no cliques. And that last fact helps to explain why the Hearts players fight so hard for each other. Few fans will remember any occasion on which a Hearts man, with the ball at his feet, didn't have several options. The back-up has been formidable.

"Character is very, very important," says Alex. "You know what they say about one rotten apple spoiling the barrel. Here it's like a family. The players like each other. They're friends on and off the park. No jealousies. No spitefulness. Of course they shout at each other, and I'm sure they fall out, now and again, but doesn't that happen in any family? When it counts, they're in there, battling for each other."

Alex was an indomitable player with Rangers. He cost Hearts £40,000, just before Wallace Mercer arrived. Sandy, he of the 1,000-plus senior matches, has five Scottish Cup badges, five League Cup and three championship medals. Both know all about pressure. Both draw heavily on their Ibrox experience, and readily admit as much.

"Pressure," says Sandy, "is when you're not playing very well, and running out in front of 30,000 people, as we did at Rangers."

"We discuss weaknesses and flaws," says Alex, "and we try to put them right. And we also know the things we do best, so that's an obvious part of tactics."

They point to the significance of the special players' lounge, a comparatively recent addition to the club. "This room means a lot," Alex says. "The players can get together here in comfort. They can watch TV, relax, have a cup of tea, just talk with their mates. And this is where we talk tactics, too. While I'm on team spirit, I should mention Jimmy Bone and Willie Johnston, by the way. They were invaluable while the new spirit was being built up."

There's a professionalism about Hearts, in the best sense of that much-abused word. Nothing proves this better than the attitude of everybody connected with the club to the fans. Pilmar Smith, one of the four directors, sees it as his duty, for instance, to liaise with the supporters, listening to their problems, working to solve these problems.

The Hearts players know and appreciate that, in the final analysis, their mortgages and their cars and their grocery bills depend on how many people pay at the Tynecastle turnstiles. You may think that such an attitude is commonplace throughout the game. You may take it for granted. You would be wrong, I'm afraid. Professional football has a fair percentage of players—and not only players—who believe the game owes them a living. Any Hearts player who even hinted at sharing that belief wouldn't last long.

In the season just finished then, Hearts attracted some of the biggest crowds in British football and there is no reason to believe they won't continue to do so. The disappointments at the death of the old season will not be forgotten, but they will be forgiven. If the atmosphere outside the Caledonian Hotel on the evening of 10 May is any guide, they have been forgiven already. If, indeed, there was anything to forgive in the first place. There were some Hearts players who feared, after the final whistle at Hampden, that they had let their fans down. They know now that nothing could have been further from the truth.

Eight days in May . . . eight days in which the title and the trophy were lost.

But the players can approach the fresh season assured that the loyalty of Hearts supporters is something very special, quite probably unequalled anywhere.

Colin McAdam was injured for the Scottish Cup Final. He watched from the stand. He told the *Express*, that weekend. "In all my years in football, I've never known anything like it. It would have been understandable if the fans had left Hampden long before the end. They stood there to a man and cheered us. It was unbelievable. We must repay them."

And Craig Levein said: "I just couldn't take it in, as we returned to Edinburgh and saw all those people out on the streets and at the hotel."

"These supporters ease the pain of it all," said John Robertson.

Naturally, every player is now more eager than ever before to WIN something they can touch and bring home next season. They talk of repaying the fans.

While any trophies will be much appreciated, I think there is something vastly more significant. Yes, we want to win, but we want to win with style and with quality. These two virtues characterised the Hearts of 1985-86, and THAT is why the fans were so unswervingly loyal. On that last Saturday they were really saying thank-you for a superb season, for thrills as much as for points, for entertainment as much as for victories.

The capacity to appreciate good football, and to scorn posers, is what a true Hearts supporter is all about. Many of the younger fans have never seen Hearts win anything, but I have no doubt that the great majority of them have developed the right outlook.

Lots of football clubs inspire the grandfather-father-son tradition of football supporting. Hearts may not have invented it. They have certainly perfected it.

The boys in maroon are the talk of the toon, all right. Long may they remain so.

PREMIER LEAGUE
1985-86

	P	W	D	L	F	A	PTS
Celtic	36	20	10	6	67	38	50
Hearts	36	20	10	6	59	33	50
Dundee Utd.	36	18	11	7	59	31	47
Aberdeen	36	16	12	8	62	31	44
Rangers	36	13	9	14	53	34	35
Dundee	36	14	7	15	45	51	35
St Mrren	36	13	5	18	42	63	31
Hibs	36	11	6	19	49	63	28
Motherwell	36	7	6	23	33	66	20
Clydebank	36	6	8	22	29	77	20

1985-86 First Team
Appearances

Substitute Appearances In Brackets

	Premier League		Skol Cup SFA Cup		Others	
	Apps	Goals	Apps	Goals	Apps	Goals
Smith	36	—	8	—	6	—
Kidd	28	—	7	1	5	1
Murray	—	—	—	—	2(1)	—
Sandison	2(1)	—	—(2)	—	1(1)	—
Cowie	7	—	1	—	—	—
Whittaker	24(1)	—	6	—	4(2)	—
Jardine (S)	35	—	8	—	5	—
Berry	32	2	5	—	4(1)5	—
MacDonald (R)	10	2	3(1)	—	3(3)	1
Levein	33	2	8	—	5	—
Mackay (G)	30(2)	3	7	2	5(1)	4
Watson	8(4)	—	3(1)	—	5(1)	2
MacDonald (A)	—(1)	—	—	—	1	—
Colquhoun	36	7	7(1)	3	5	—
Robertson	34(1)	20	8	5	5(1)	5
Clark	33	12	7	—	5	1
McNaughton	2(2)	—	1	1	1(3)	2
Black	23(6)	2	7	1	3(3)	1
Cherry	3(2)	—	—(2)	1	—	—
Jardine (I)	19(3)	7	1(1)	—	1	—
McDermott	—	—	—	—	(1)	—
McAdam	—(5)	—	—(1)	1	—(1)	—
Mckay (W)	—(3)	—	—(1)	—	—	—